"Eleven years after his death, Padre Pio is still remembered and loved by millions of people the world over. During his life thousands of these same people were direct recipients of his intercession and pastoral care, and stories of his miracles and cures abound.

"The stories in this book are told by a man who at first didn't want anything to do with the superstitious business of wonderworking, but who himself was cured by Padre Pio. They represent only those facts of which the author had personal knowledge or experience. . . .

"McCaffery tells of Padre Pio's curing blindness, cancer, and other diseases, as well as restoring spirit and courage to all who came to him. There comes through, in addition, the monk's character as a warm human being. The simple manner in which the stories are told is perhaps their main strength: no frantic attempt to prove miraculous powers, but a relaxed certainty and an inviting style.

"A somewhat different treatment of the life of an extraordinary man."

Spiritual Book News, Jan./Feb. 1980

T0137919

TALES OF
PADRE PIO

TALES OF
PADRE PIO

The Friar of San Giovanni

by
JOHN McCAFFERY

IMAGE BOOKS
A Division of Doubleday & Company, Inc.
Garden City, New York

Image Books edition published September 1981
by special arrangement with Andrews and McMeel, Inc.

First published in Great Britain in 1978
by Darton, Longman & Todd Ltd.,
under the title *The Friar of San Giovanni*.

ISBN-13: 978-0-385-17739-9
ISBN: 0-385-17739-9
Library of Congress Catalog Card Number 81-43068
Copyright © 1978 by John McCaffery
Printed in the United States of America

INTRODUCTORY NOTE

Padre Pio was an Italian Capuchin monk born in 1887 of poor peasant parents in the southern Italian village of Pietralcina. He died in 1968 in a remote minor monastery of his Order at San Giovanni Rotondo, in the province of Foggia, where he had passed the last fifty years of his life.

Normally no one should ever have heard of him. Instead, drawn by his stigmata and by his extraordinary powers of spiritual and physical healing, literally millions of people made their way to that little monastery from every corner of the globe. His name today is known and venerated throughout the world.

This book is in no sense a biography. It is merely a collection of simple stories drawn chiefly from personal contacts with Padre Pio and with those surrounding him. Should any of the facts which it contains seem astounding or incredible, let me say that, restricted as they are to personal knowledge or experience, they represent only a very small tip of a very large iceberg. The miracles wrought by Padre Pio, attested by people who themselves or members of whose families were at the receiving end of them, run into thousands, or more probably tens of thousands.

Many of them are described in those biographies and other publications which have appeared in several languages, and the magazine published at San

Giovanni Rotondo under the auspices of Padre Pio's hospital has of late been carrying a wealth of direct testimonies from its wide circle of readers.

The full extent of Padre Pio's authentic miracles will, however, never be known. They span half a century and cover all parts of the world. Most of them are destined to remain unrecorded.

But the example and spiritual splendor of his life is there for all to see. And that life, his attributes, and those works which we know constitute a tremendous rebuttal of all the blind and stupidly presumptuous godlessness of our present age.

I have written down these reminiscences in the hope that those who read them will be moved to find out more about Padre Pio and will give him the opportunity of carrying on and extending through them the crusade of leavening and succor to which his life and sufferings, like those of his Master, were wholly dedicated.

They have been written entirely from memory. It is therefore possible, because of the passage of time, that where there is not direct personal experience there may be circumstantial details which are not completely accurate; but for the factual occurrence of all the events and episodes herein recounted I can vouch absolutely.

J. McC.

CHAPTER I

One evening I was on a train going from Bologna to Rome and fell into conversation with a youngish man who was sitting opposite me in the Pullman car. It transpired that he was a farmer from near Padua, that he employed about sixty people, and that he had won the national cup for wheat production the previous year.

At the time I too was an aspiring, part-time farmer, and while people around us on this businessman's express were discussing letters of credit, import licenses and the like, we were having a fascinating exchange of views on things like the comparative values of farmyard and artificial manures, rotational grazing on stock farms, and similar earthy topics.

He asked me whether I was coming back directly from Rome to my business base in Milan, and I said no, I was going farther south. Might he ask where? Well, to a little place he had probably never heard of called San Giovanni Rotondo. (In those days it had not yet become famous, even inside Italy.)

He looked at me, took out his wallet, produced a photograph, and said "Is that him?" I took out my own wallet, produced my own photograph, and replied "Indeed it is!" We both laughed heartily, and I asked him "Have you been down there?" "Seven times," he replied; and then, after a pause, "You see, I had a miraculous cure through him, before I even knew of his existence."

Now, in those days "miraculous" in connection with Padre Pio was a term to be avoided. One dared not use it in ecclesiastical circles, for Mother Church was playing true to form and, like the old Scots lady whom the minister observed in church bowing her head each time Satan's name was mentioned, she was averring, "Well, you never know!" Mother Church tends to recognize her saints only when they are dead, when their free wills are no longer operative.

However, those of us who had the extreme privilege of personal contact with Padre Pio realized more fully than most that saints become such during their lifetimes, not after death, and that God is never outdone in generosity; and we had seen too many authentic miracles to have any doubts about them. But this was something new; to have been miraculously cured by him while still unaware of his existence was something I had never yet come across. And here was the story.

On his farm one day, not long after the end of the war, this man had a very serious accident, the outcome of which was a double embolism, one on each lung. They filled him up, as he related, with the new drugs, and these seemed to work for a while; but then the embolisms came back worse than ever, and he realized that he was going to die.

He was young and strong, and he did not want to go yet. He was also religious and intelligent; and he prayed to God in a way I had never heard of anyone's praying before. "I asked God with all the supplication I could muster," he said, "to let someone more worthy than I intercede for me." It was an extraordinary prayer, and it had an extraordinary answer.

"I had," he told me, "what I can only describe as an apparition. There was a bearded monk by my bedside. He bent forward and laid his hand on my chest, smiled, and then disappeared."

He felt immediately that he had been cured, and, to the amazement of the doctors, this was fully confirmed. But he told no one of his "apparition" excepting his mother, "because," he explained, "people would have thought I was mentally deranged or neurotic." So his mother and he kept "the secret of the king," and left the doctors and others to their hypotheses.

They both wondered who was the monk in the case and concluded, naturally enough, that he must be some great saint of the past.

Thus several months passed, until one morning he was in Padua doing business with a man who afterward invited him home to lunch.

"As I entered the living room," he said, "I was transfixed. For there on the wall was, not a picture, but a photograph of the monk who had appeared to me!" He asked his host who it was, and, dynamic character that he was, the reply, with the accounts of Padre Pio that he heard over lunch, saw him on the train for Foggia that very evening.

He arrived there around four in the morning, bemused by the suddenness and strangeness of his journey, found a taxi outside the station, and was at the little church just in time for Padre Pio's five o'clock Mass.

"When he came out onto the altar," he told me,

"I had no doubts left. This was most certainly the monk who had appeared in response to my prayer."

It was midwinter, and there were not the throngs which later descended upon San Giovanni Rotondo all the year round. Instead of having to wait for several days to go to confession, the easiest way to hold converse with him, he was able to go that same day.

"Here and now in the train," he said, "I relive, I assure you, all the emotion of that moment. He blessed me, and I made my confession. And then, at the end of it he said to me with the most natural voice in the world, 'And tell me, what about the lungs now? How are they?' 'Thank you, Father,' I answered him, 'they are perfect.' 'Have you had them X-rayed?' 'Yes, Father.' 'Good. Thanks be to God. And God bless you.'

"Do you wonder," he asked me, "that I keep going down to San Giovanni? Or that it gives me goose flesh to recount these things to you even now?"

CHAPTER II

Strangely enough, the next tale that comes to mind begins also upon a train, this time the one for Foggia already mentioned. How many people have taken that train, weighed down with the whole variety of ills to which flesh is heir, and gone back into the world cleansed and transformed.

It was after one of my frequent visits to Rome. Five Scottish priests, old friends, had come there to celebrate the silver jubilee of their ordination. I had spent a very pleasant morning with them and, in order to expand it to its fullest extent, had said I would take lunch on the one-thirty train south. Alas, there was no dining car; but there was a trolley with eatables and drinkables and, hearing it approach, I went out into the corridor.

A diminutive American lady was not making much headway in explaining her requirements to the attendant, so I offered to interpret, and we stood then to take our coffee and sandwiches together.

She asked me whether this particular portion of the train went to Naples. "No," I told her, "you will have to change to another coach. This one is going to Foggia." "Oh, but that is the one I want," said she, "so that's fine."

With all due respect to Foggia, what American lady would want to go there unless to proceed somewhere else? It is a large, busy market and industrial town, but it has little tourist pull, and its international links are restricted.

"You are not, by any chance, going to San Giovanni Rotondo, are you?" I asked her. She looked at me with amazement. "Are you going there too?" "I am." "Now isn't that just something?" she said. "Because, in answer to your question, I just don't know whether I am going to San Giovanni Rotondo or not. I am liable to get off the train before we get there.

"You see," she continued, "this is my last, my only desperate chance; and I am terrified of being disappointed."

At that point the train entered a tunnel, and she said, "Do you see this dark tunnel?" "Yes." "Well, that's my life." And then: "Do you see that little glimmer of light where we shall be coming out?" "Yes." "That is Padre Pio. He is the only spark of hope left to me, and if he fails me, my life is in ruins. I have come five thousand miles, all the way from Hawaii, to see him. But, in my fear of putting him to the test, I have been sitting for three weeks in a Rome hotel. Yesterday I went to Mass at the American church of Santa Susanna, and in the course of his sermon the priest said, 'Let me tell you a story recounted by Padre Pio, the stigmatist.' When he had finished the story, I said to myself, 'That's a jog on the elbow for you,' and so this morning I threw some things into a grip, came to the station, and here I am. But, as I told you, I am absolutely terrified, and could leave the train before we reach Foggia."

"You won't," I said to her, "because I won't let you. Are you a Catholic?" "*Was,*" she replied. "If

you were, and you are now on your way to Padre
Pio, then you still are. Put away your worries and
your fears. And don't believe this is a casual encounter. I have seen too many 'chance episodes' like
this. Padre Pio has most definitely placed me in your
path. He has followed every step of your journey;
and he is waiting for you."

There were four hours or so to go before we
reached our destination, and for three of those I sat
and spoke to her of Padre Pio, his human warmth
and compassion, and the marvelous things I had
seen or knew of. Eventually she asked me, "Can I
go to confession to him?" "No," I told her, "he
hears confessions only in Italian. But there is an
American friar there called Father Dominic, and
you can go to him. I shall introduce you to him and
then leave you to your own devices; because every
pilgrim must find his or her own San Giovanni.
Your problems you can relate to him, and let him
pass them on. And if you feel you want to speak to
me or to ask me anything, you know that I am there
and always available."

For the last hour I spoke to her of Father Dominic and what a good, kindly man he was; of how
he had been cured of cancer by Padre Pio; and of
how (which will make another tale) his father had
been assisted by Padre Pio in bi-location on his
deathbed in Milwaukee. I was still speaking of him
when the train drew into Foggia.

Outside I got a taxi for us both and left the driver
to stow the luggage in the trunk. When he had done
so, he opened the door and said, "Excuse me, sir.
One of the friars from San Giovanni has just come

off the train. Would you like to give him a lift?" "By all means. Ask him to come over."

Yes, it was Father Dominic. When I introduced him, my traveling companion literally changed color. "Do you believe me now that Padre Pio has been following every step of your journey?" "Oh, indeed I do!" she replied in a very small voice.

"Father," I said, "we have been talking about you for the last hour. Pardon my asking you so crudely, but did Padre Pio cure you of cancer?" Father Dominic beamed his beatific beam. "Yes, he did," he replied, "and I have just been having my annual checkup. I know they won't find anything—but it gets me a week's break in Rome!"

Three quarters of an hour it takes a car to rise and wind from Foggia up to the red, rocky hills of San Giovanni Rotondo, to the "city set upon a mountain." During that time I encouraged Father Dominic to tell his countrywoman, much better than I had been able to, the amazing things she had heard recently on the train. When we arrived, she was a very well-informed neophyte indeed, and also a much calmer woman.

Next day, however, her calm was somewhat broken—but happily so. She came hurrying over to me in the hotel lounge and said, "I've been looking for you. I even went and banged on your door!" "Why?" "I got the perfume," she replied.

Of this perfume I shall speak shortly, but here let it suffice to say she was referring to that beautiful perfume by which Padre Pio manifested his invisible presence, his interest or approval, or by which he gave some message he wished to convey, at San Giovanni or at the ends of the earth.

"I was standing in my room lost in thought," she recounted, "when suddenly I became aware of a strong, exquisite perfume. Strange, I wondered. I did not pack any. I looked in my grip, in the chest of drawers, all over the room. Nothing; and the scent had become still stronger. All at once I knew what it was. The perfume of Padre Pio, of which I had heard—this was it! And that was when I ran from my room and banged on your door!"

That evening I spoke of the incident to Father Dominic; and when I told him, in reply to his question, at what time it had occurred, he said, "Well, he was certainly quick off the mark. I had just spoken to him of the lady and her problems." What he should have said, of course, was "quick off the mark tactically as well as strategically," since this was only the latest episode in the long chain stretching from here back to Hawaii.

I got to know this extremely fine-drawn American woman fairly well during my short stay; well enough to realize, among other things, what a vast amount of courage went into small compass. I naturally asked her nothing about her personal problems but presumed, perhaps wrongly, that they were matrimonial. Anyway, she was still there when I left, and since she said she wanted to visit the Holy House of Loreto and my train stopped at Loreto, we did that bit of the journey together. I shall always remember the lonely-looking little figure, with courage in its every line, standing waving good-by on an empty platform as the train moved out.

Shortly after Christmas that year I received an envelope from the States. It contained a promise of continuous remembrance of my family and myself.

But the real substance of the letter was: "It is Christmas Eve. For the first time in eleven years I am able to go to Midnight Mass and to Holy Communion; and I shall be praying for Padre Pio, for Father Dominic, and for you." God bless her. That was a very happy moment. She had come out at last from her tunnel.

CHAPTER III

And now, to hark back, what of the perfume? One had, of course, heard of "the odor of sanctity." The biographers of saints often said they had died in it; and it was generally a noble metaphor. Not so, however, in the case of Padre Pio.

Did I ever experience it? Time and again, alone, in company, in San Giovanni and far away from it—but always completely unexpectedly, and therefore with no possibility of autosuggestion. It generally conveyed a message but sometimes was just like an affectionate pat on the head.

One of the earliest occasions I remember was when Padre Pio was hearing confessions in the small church and I was standing among the crowd of people who would remain there, standing or kneeling, to share his presence until he re-entered the monastery. Suddenly I felt this powerful wave of captivating perfume, and my first reaction was to think, "Good God, what unspeakable female has soaked herself like that in expensive scent before coming here?" As I gazed around, however, I saw people look at each other with comprehending smiles and heard one girl say to her companion, "That is the fourth time I have felt the perfume this morning."

On another early occasion the perfume came to me individually in the little church as a kind of reward, I felt, for my boy-scoutish "good deed for the day."

I had arrived at the church door well before dawn, long before it opened, and had secured for myself an excellent vantage point whence to be able to see Padre Pio at close quarters throughout his Mass at the altar of St. Francis. Just as he was about to emerge from the sacristy, I noticed the good Padre Vincenzo, monastery porter, or keeper of the door, come out to celebrate Mass at another side altar without having anybody to serve it for him. There was a sharp conflict, but I brought myself to surrender the vantage point I had risen so early to obtain; and when Padre Vincenzo reached the moment of consecration, out from nowhere welled again that tremendous perfume. It was the most fantastic pat on the head or back I have ever received; a proof that, if I was unable to follow Padre Pio's Mass, my own puny sacrifice had been duly followed by him.

Several times the perfume conveyed a clear, unmistakable message. In one instance it came out almost imperiously when I was showing Leonardo's *Last Supper* to an acquaintance, not a Catholic, but a very dedicated Christian. He was a man who, for example, boarded or tried to board Soviet ships in London docks with copies of the Bible in Russian. But my link with him was purely a business one, and as we gazed at the great fresco I was debating within myself whether or not it was appropriate to "give" him Padre Pio to take back to England with him. Out came the wave of perfume! And I knew then that indeed it was.

I do not know to what extent, if at all, it developed afterward, but his reaction outside the church when I spoke to him of Padre Pio was most striking. Before he accepted the initial description of this miracle-working stigmatist, he looked me straight in the eye for about twenty seconds. It is a long time in the circumstances; and he was seeking to gauge my seriousness and balance—very understandably, since the Middle Ages were long buried, were they not, and the buses were running past in Corso Magenta.

Another message came during lunch in Savini's restaurant in Milan's Galleria. This time too it concerned an English business acquaintance, who, I knew, had been going through a very rough domestic time. He also was not a Catholic, and again I wondered whether I could possibly "give" him Padre Pio, just like that, between one course and another, to provide him with some consolation and hope. There it was again, the presence of that strong, penetrating perfume, an odor completely divorced from *osso buco* or *riso al salto,* or any other of the delectable dishes that the Savini chefs are wont to produce. Once more I knew that Padre Pio was there and what he wanted, and I duly obliged.

This man showed immediately just how much he needed him, and how much he was in tune. He opened his soul to the Padre Pio story like a parched flower to the summer rain; and it seemed to me that never again would he feel quite so hurt or quite so lonely as he had been hitherto.

Did Padre Pio himself ever have anything to say of the perfume? He described it once, when questioned, as "just sweets for the children"!

CHAPTER IV

On commencing this book, it seemed to me a good idea to plunge right into the tales at once without any personalized introduction. However, it would be strange not to relate how I got to know Padre Pio.

I spoke a moment ago of "a miracle-working stigmatist." Nowadays the world knows about Padre Pio and has been able—too easily indeed—to absorb him. But then, before his fame had spread, what other reaction could anyone normally have than incredulity or suspended judgment? My own reaction was perhaps even stronger, for I had always loved the rationality of the Church and had on occasion been accused of being "too cerebral a Catholic"; I wanted no part of some sort of mystic operating in the depths of southern Italy.

It began during the Second World War, when I was trying to organize and support the European resistance movements from a base in Switzerland. Equally peculiarly, my confessor was an enemy subject, preposterous though the term seems for such a simple, saintly old man. It was just that I spoke Italian better than French or German, and English-speaking confessors were thin on the ground.

Don Rizzi ran the Italian mission in Bern, and though he looked almost a figure of fun against the Bern background, cycling slowly around town in his Roman clerical hat and his long black cloak, he was a good and dear friend to me in a basic world where war and enemy subjects just did not exist. He also spoke to me about Padre Pio and gave me a book concerning him. I flicked through the pages and did not even trouble to read it.

At the end of the war, the man burdened with my problems of conscience in Milan was a Capuchin who, red-cheeked and white-bearded, looked like a small edition of Father Christmas. Padre Gian Antonio still could not believe he was alive. He had survived two years of Dachau for helping people to escape the Nazi net and get across the Swiss frontier. And he too spoke to me of Padre Pio, giving me two small photographs instead of a book. These too elicited only polite evasion.

Then came Douglas Woodruff. Anyone conversant with middle-of-the-century literary and political Britain knows that he was one of its luminaries. It seemed to me incredible that he too should be a believer, and a very convinced believer, in Padre Pio.

Still I was not persuaded. But my curiosity was very much aroused; and when Piero Pellizzari, son of an old and distinguished Italian friend, appeared one day bubbling over with enthusiasm for Padre Pio and asking me to go down to San Giovanni with him, I consented to go, but still full of reluctance, constraint, and clad in an armor of quasi-hostility.

It all evaporated with his Mass, his marvelous Mass, at which I was assisting for the first time on a St. Patrick's morning. This was a literal revelation. And when, in the evening, Dr. Sanguinetti led me to Padre Pio's cell and I found myself in that warm, sincere, and uniquely saintly presence, I could have flung myself straightway at his feet. For "virtue went out from him," and I felt at once what years of experience only confirmed, that I was looking on one of the greatest saints the world had ever seen.

Poor old St. Thomas the Apostle, he who was to go down in history as Doubting Thomas. I felt I could understand his feelings when he was invited to touch Our Saviour's wounds.

CHAPTER V

However, having "seen and touched" Padre Pio, I did at least try to make up for lost time.

They were great days, those, before the big church was built and the monastery expanded, and when the flow of people—especially during the winter months—was not so intense.

Padre Pio's lay collaborators had easy access to the monastery, and they had in any case an evening conference with him lasting for half or three quarters of an hour in the monastery parlor every day. Entry was often permitted to priests who had come from any distance, or to laymen with some special motive which the Father Porter considered adequate.

In my own case, I found the most facile entry obtainable was by being on friendly terms with as many of the friars as possible and asking to see, not Padre Pio, but one of them! They were so very kind and understanding that, realizing perfectly well it was chiefly a ruse to get in touch with Padre Pio, they would come down, take me up to their cells for a chat, and then lead me along the corridor to wait until he should appear.

Often, however, I would arrange to go in with Dr. Sanguinetti, or with Giovanni Vignolini, the infirmarian; and eventually I became sufficiently known at the *Portineria* to go in alone. That was a great day.

It might seem an extraordinary thing that a monastery should be invaded by outsiders, chiefly laymen. But, apart from the fact that it was no ordinary monastery, this happened only during certain specific hours of the day. Otherwise it stood there quiet and withdrawn. And, of course, with a person of Padre Pio's unique sanctity and force of character to guide and assist the Guardian, whoever he might be, there was never any question of the situation's getting out of hand.

We waited for him inside and outside the monastery, in his own corridor, in the passage between monastery and church, in the sacristy before and after his Masses, his Benedictions, and his distributions of Holy Communion. And we were content with a glance, a word, a passing blessing, or to touch his garment. A very fortunate few—and I was lucky enough to become one of them—were able to be in the "Choir" (the gallery or choir loft used by the Community) during ceremonies and to share the stalls with the friars; or even, a mighty privilege indeed, with him. That was something worth taking back to the outside world.

And yet, I must say a surprising thing. Of those "Choir" days, the incidents that stand out most clearly in my mind will always fill me with laughter.

Isn't that astonishing in connection with one than whom no human being ever suffered more, who had all the sorrows of the world brought to him? And of the spot where he received the stigmata, where one could now witness his intense, concentrated colloquy with his Divine Lord? In fact all my memories of

Padre Pio are permeated by humor more than by anything else.

Yet perhaps it is not so strange; for happiness and joy have always been characteristics of genuine sanctity, as though it saw through the true and transient nature of suffering to the end product in eternity.

Anyway, unless of course when he was obviously undergoing exceptional pain or distress, or when the circumstances clearly did not warrant it, I could never see Padre Pio without his evoking a spontaneous smile. And that still holds good today. Before me, above the mantelpiece in my study, is a large, very lifelike portrait of him done by Ciccone, the boy who grew up in San Giovanni Rotondo and, with Padre Pio's help, became one of the world's well-known painters.* It regularly sparks off the same affectionate grin; and when at times things go wrong for me, I look through it to himself and, humorously if possible, protest!

* I have before me now an announcement of Antonio Ciccone's latest exhibition in New York. His brief biography contained therein is as follows: "Antonio Ciccone was born in San Giovanni Rotondo, Foggia, Italy, on January 15, 1939. At the age of fourteen he was sent to study for seven years at the Art Schools of Annigoni and Simi under the guidance and sustained interest of Padre Pio of Pietralcina. Antonio Ciccone has executed many frescoes in churches and private homes and has received numerous commissions for portraits in both pencil and oil. He has been the recipient of many awards and his exhibitions include twenty one-man shows in Europe and the United States. Antonio Ciccone now lives and works in Southampton (N.Y.) and Florence, Italy, with his wife, the former Linda Merrill, and their six children. Long familiar to residents and visitors to Southampton for his fine oil portraits and figurative drawings, Antonio Ciccone has recently completed a series of exciting oil landscapes of eastern Long Island."

The "Choir" incidents I speak of would indeed have been simple things but for the personality of their protagonist.

The first, which took place not in the "Choir" itself but in a small room adjoining it, lay in the spectacle (humorous only in retrospect) of Dr. Sanguinetti, Padre Pio's favorite son, his chief agent in the important hospital project, being given a furious dressing down by him and being then ordered downstairs to the public church below.

Dr. Sanguinetti was heavily burdened with the problems of the hospital then going up, and of the news sheet he was launching to keep friends in touch and help raise funds. On the way to the "Choir" he suggested that my companion and myself should finish discussing some of those problems with him now, since we were leaving that evening, and that we should proceed to the "Choir" only in time for Padre Pio's giving Benediction. This meant missing the sermon being delivered by one of the other friars, and taking one's cue from the Litany of Loreto which Mary Pyle's village-girl choristers would be singing at the end of it.

The cue never materialized. Instead, an irate Padre Pio appeared in the doorway and apostrophized us for sitting there talking instead of listening to the preacher. We were shattered by his onslaught. "You two," he said, indicating Piero Pellizzari and myself, "I would shoot! But you," turning to Dr. Sanguinetti, "I would boil in oil for giving such bad example! Now get down at once to the church!"

There was to be no "Choir" for us that day. After his departure, the tough-grained doctor recovered his spirits somewhat and said, "It's all very well. He talks about giving bad example. But I just cannot listen to Father So-and-So's sermons without going to sleep. And when I sleep, I snore. And that is even worse example! Let's go down to church as he has bidden us but not through the sacristy, where he is vesting. He has not finished with me yet, and I don't relish taking the rest of it in public!"

After Benediction, and before Piero and I left, we went quietly in with the others for the evening talk— rather dubiously on my part, I must confess. But Padre Pio's ire had by this time subsided, and all we got from him was an eloquent, minatory "H'mm!"

The episode, with the passage of time, rather like a school prank involving the headmaster, became funnier than ever for the participants, and many a time was the doctor's chastisement mirthfully recalled during later visits.

The other incident took place in the "Choir" itself on a Sunday morning. There were times when, on arriving at San Giovanni and seeing Padre Pio come out to say Mass, I would say to myself, "I've got here just in time. He is about to die." He would be deathly pale, drawn, barely able to drag himself along. Then, meeting him later in the day, I would find a complete metamorphosis, and he would seem as bright and cheerful as a young novice. This was one of his really bad mornings.

The custom had arisen that on Sundays, when generally there were more pilgrims, he would appear at the "Choir" window at midday, bless the crowd gathered on the *piazza* below, and say the Angelus with them. On this particular Sunday there were more than fifty busloads of people, besides all those who had come by car, taxi, and on foot. The *piazza* was packed and colorful in the sunshine, and there rose from it a great, swelling murmur of expectancy. Padre Pio entered the "Choir" accompanied by that faithful acolyte, Padre Eusebio, whom he loved as Christ loved St. John, and of whom much more anon.

He was obviously in very great pain and hardly able to walk. His face was ashen. Padre Eusebio clearly was worried, but there he was talking cheerfully and jestingly to Padre Pio as he helped him along. Generally he could rouse him to a smile as no one else could; but not this time. For who knows what or whose reason, he was plunged in the depths.

Padre Eusebio, however, kept up his quiet, brisk flow of remarks and began to help him into his surplice. In doing so he ruffled Padre Pio's hair, and as the latter began to move slowly and painfully toward the window, he exclaimed, "No, not yet! Just a moment!" and took out a small comb from the pocket of his habit. Poor Padre Pio stood there like a child while his hair was adjusted, and then Padre Eusebio stood back with a great, affectionate smile and said, "On you go now, Padre! You are the image of St. Anthony!"

Padre Pio gave one of those spontaneous, subdued snorts of laughter at such cheek, braced himself, and went forward to embrace the waiting crowd with that warm, fatherly blessing which each person accepted as though given individually to himself or herself—as indeed it was.

CHAPTER VI

How can one say that each person in the crowd received an individual, personal blessing?

It was as though, for his having identified himself with the suffering Christ, God had given Padre Pio some small participation in his omniscience and ubiquity—or had anyhow freed him of this world's three-dimensional fetters.

Speaking one day of his continuous and often necessarily simultaneous contacts with a number of persons in different places, someone said he supposed it was on the same principle as tuning in with a radio. But I asked him what would happen if one attempted to transmit and receive at the same time, or even tried to tune in simultaneously to several different stations. It was all very different.

Again, to take my own experience, he would poke fun at me by telling me what I had been thinking of the previous evening, or what my program was for the coming week, or what I had been discussing so confidentially with the Father Guardian in his cell! He seemed to know everything. But not only personal or immediate things. Though he did not read a newspaper or spend his time before radio or television, he could discuss international politics with full cognizance of personalities and events, and I well remember some of his highly original and perceptive judgments.

Concerning an internationally known figure who was extremely able, but unfortunately corrupt, I said one day, "Padre, think of the good he could accomplish if he had the right ideas. Shall I try to get him down here so that you can make him change his life?" We were standing talking in an alcove of his monastery corridor and, for the only time ever, he just did not answer but looked silently out of the window. Some weeks later the man in question was assassinated.

Carlo Campanini was one of Italy's leading comedians, and he was deeply attached to Padre Pio. When he was not engaged in the theater he would spend long periods at San Giovanni, and Padre Pio loved his ready wit. Furthermore, and to illustrate again how affection for Padre Pio was often shot through with laughter, Campanini could leave us helpless with his humorous imitations of him when Padre Pio was himself displaying the witty or ironical or even angry side of his character.

On one occasion Padre Pio was ill during Campanini's visit, and our good friend was sitting by his bedside when one of the friars brought in a stack of envelopes and packages upon which people requested his blessing. "Will you bless these, Padre?" asked the friar. "Yes," he replied, "but not that envelope there."

As the friar left, Campanini, consumed with curiosity, respectfully suggested he should tire Padre Pio no further, and followed him. A group was gathered around the door giving onto the entrance corridor, and as each envelope or package was held up, it was duly claimed by its owner. Finally, only the rejected envelope was left. "Whose is this?" asked the friar.

"Mine!" replied a strong Neapolitan accent. "Padre Pio has refused to bless it." Sensation in the audience, and Campanini was all eyes and ears. "Ah, well," said the outlaw with an impudent grin, "one can only try." He removed a piece of paper and held it up for inspection. It was his football-pools coupon for the week!

I could go on for a long time with tales of Padre Pio's preternatural knowledge or prophetic vision; but let me end with an episode in utter contrast, alas, with the above.

The last time I saw my old friend Dr. Sanguinetti was when he was setting up the farm that was to supply the hospital with milk and eggs, fruit and vegetables. I had spent several very happy evenings with his wife and him and had already taken farewell of them on the eve of my departure. But then, as the moment approached to go and say good-by to Padre Pio, I was affected by a scruple and went down first to the farm.

"*Dottore,*" I said, "I should hate you to think that, because I can now find my own way into the monastery unaided, I have forgotten who it was that first led me in and made me, as it were, one of the family. Let us go up again now together." The doctor assured me he would never have had any such unworthy thought, but his warm heart was touched, and he came with me.

We met Padre Pio near his cell and talked at length with him. At last it was time to leave, but whereas generally it was I who tried to prolong the conversation, this time it was he who seemed unwilling to end it. The car to take me to Foggia was by now waiting below, and twice I had vainly

attempted to go. Finally, I decided that if he wished
me to miss the train there was certainly some good
reason for it, so I relaxed and carried on talking.

When eventually I received the farewell embrace
and parting blessing, there was not the slightest
chance of making Foggia in time, and I said this at
once to the driver. "Just get in, sir," he said. "The
train stops for one minute at San Severo, farther up
the line, and we shall manage to cut across there
and catch it." This was stop-press news to me; but
evidently not to Padre Pio!

However, I got on that train a very thoughtful
man; because, before letting me go, he had given a
long look at Dr. Sanguinetti and myself and had
said: "Who knows when and where we shall meet
again?" Another friend waiting to speak to him had
overheard this and, breaking in, said, "But Mr.
McCaffery is coming back here in September."
"Yes," he replied, "I know."

Now there was only one reason why I was still
around and walking the earth. Padre Pio had obtained for me an extension of my allotted time, and
I shall speak of this in due course. The deduction
now seemed obvious to me that my borrowed time
must be up. The *dottore* was the picture of robust
health, sturdy as the proverbial oak. Also he had not
yet finished the hospital. But six weeks later I got a
telegram from San Giovanni announcing his sudden
death from a heart attack.

"Unlike us, God saw that he was ready," said
Padre Pio.

CHAPTER VII

"*Il dottore*" must have received an extremely warm welcome when God called him home, because for long years he had been the shield, the staff, the unflagging support of one of God's most precious creatures. Padre Pio knew he could count upon him entirely in all things. His affection and his loyalty were absolute; he never refused a task; and his sincerity and spontaneity were such that he felt no constriction or shyness in Padre Pio's presence, such as most of us felt to a greater or lesser degree, so that Padre Pio could relax in his company as he could do with very few other persons.

He cared for no man breathing, except Padre Pio; and for no woman, except his gentle, charming wife, the Signora Emilia, whom he loved devotedly. This latter great light of his life had led him to the other.

He was a country doctor, bluff and forthright, whom one could imagine his patients worshiping for his dedication and blunt good humor; and he must have enjoyed his rural life among them. There were only two shadows. Some unhappy experience he had had with the ecclesiastical world had disgusted him, and he had become anti-clerical. This, and the fact that no children had been born to them, constituted two heavy crosses for the Signora Emilia. She decided that she would make one major attempt to eliminate the first of them, and she did not realize that, in the spiritual order, she was thereby also going to eliminate the second, and create for them a family that would be vast, demanding, and greatly recompensing.

As each wedding anniversary approached, the doctor would ask his beloved "Mi" what she would most like as a present. On this particular occasion she took her courage in both hands and said, "A trip together to see Padre Pio!" Her husband was dumfounded. "No, no, Mi," he exclaimed, "that is not fair." And then, being the man he was and loving her as he did, "Sorry, Mi, I take it back. If that's what you want, that's what it is."

They came to San Giovanni for their wedding anniversary, and the inevitable happened. This tough, prejudiced man looked into the eyes of Padre Pio and saw there something he had never seen before in his life. He gave in without a struggle.

After his confession and Communion he knew that his life-style was going to change; but he had not remotely realized by just how much.

Padre Pio told him of his desire to create a large hospital here in this poverty-stricken, primitive, forgotten region. And then came the bombshell. "You, *Dottore,* are the man who will come here and build it." Dr. Sanguinetti looked at him in amazement. "But," he said, "I am a doctor, a country doctor. You need an architect or an engineer." "Not at all. It is you who will build it. You will see." "But, Padre, even if I had the qualifications, I still could not do it, for the only money I have is what I earn by my profession." "That," rejoined Padre Pio, "will be taken care of."

When, a couple of months later, one of the doctor's premium bonds drew quite a large sum of money in the national bond lottery, he knew exactly why, and what was now demanded of him. With part of the money he purchased an agricultural property not far from Florence and rented it out to provide himself with an income. With the rest he built his new house at San Giovanni and began to organize the construction of the hospital.

"Si monumentum quaeris, circumspice." The great, pale, noble hospital is not just Padre Pio's monument but, at least in human effort, his too. So too are the green slopes above the hospital, church, and monastery, where he planted and staked thousand upon thousand of trees to cover the barrenness of the red, rocky hillside.

A Milanese architect, and a romantic, who once came down to San Giovanni in my company, said as he looked at the tall dark green cypresses encircling the monastery garden, "How contrasting! Why, this is a little corner of his own Umbria that St. Francis has dropped upon these stony heights!" So likewise did Guglielmo Sanguinetti find time to create the green hillside above it; and up through his trees the pilgrims now wend their way as they follow those Stations of the Cross sculpted strikingly in bronze by that other famous disciple of Padre Pio's, Francesco Messina.

As he gazed upon the wilderness and isolation, Dr. Sanguinetti must have needed all his new-found faith to embark upon his gigantic task. He had helpers, yes: there came Angelo Lupi, the architectural genius who designed the hospital in its imposing yet functional proportions; Carlo Kisvarday, accountant; Massimiliano Malaguti, who, among other things, conceived the prolific idea of "lighting a star" in the Padre Pio firmament by gifting a bed; other willing souls, whose numbers grew. And there were earnest men elsewhere like Giovanni Sacchetti and Bernardo Patrizi, those two uncharacteristic Roman nobles, and Mario Sanvico of Perugia, who worked hard in various ways to make Padre Pio's dream a reality.

But, at the beginning, the whole immense project in such an unlikely setting must have seemed quixotic and almost certainly doomed to failure. Excepting, of course, for the quality of the man behind it all; and Padre Pio soon began to give his recently acquired friend further demonstration of what that meant.

A Hospital Fund was established, and straightway money began to flow in from the most unexpected quarters. Innumerable tales could be told of how that money turned up. No matter how much against the laws of probability it might seem, it was always there in time to meet the needs of the moment.

Like so many similar charitable institutions, the hospital grew up on faith. But faith without good works is void; and if Padre Pio supplied the faith and the potential, Guglielmo Sanguinetti was there to look after the works. He drove trucks, he drove men, but above all he drove himself. Nothing was beyond or below his competence. He learned a host of new skills, found himself technical advisers and consultants, became expert in wedding economy to solidity and dignity in the choice of materials. In the matter of ensuring there would be no exploitation in quality of goods or in costs, he was like a tiger.

Padre Pio insisted that those monies which

poured in were sacred. Some came in large amounts, more in moderate donations, and a very great deal in the widow's mites of the poor. The foundations of the Fund had been laid by Emanuele Brunatto, one of Padre Pio's earliest devotees, who will appear later in these pages. Barbara Ward (now Lady Jackson), the English Catholic writer and economist, did a great deal for it, and through her enterprise and initiative a very substantial early contribution was obtained as a memorial tribute to Fiorello la Guardia, former Mayor of New York. The Fund for the Sick Poor, however, was named after a poor expatriate Italian worker, Mario Gambino, behind whose modest contribution Padre Pio knew what sacrifices lay.

A famous offering was that of a little fifty-lira note. This Padre Pio kept in the pocket of his habit and would produce it, sometimes with tears, as he told the story of it. It had been offered to him by a poor widow of the district, and he had at first refused it, saying that she could not afford it and that it was not expected of her. She insisted and said she could make small economies by, for instance, not buying matches and obtaining from neighbors a light for her fire and her lamp. When he still refused, she said resignedly, "Well, yes, Padre, I suppose it is too small." That was when Padre Pio first wept. "Give it to me!" he answered. "Give it to me at once! It is the handsomest donation I have yet received." And so the little note became a symbol, a reminder to those collaborating with him in the launching of the hospital, of the care and respect with which the monies at their disposal should be handled.

The solid, determined figure of Dr. Sanguinetti

played the principal part for so long on the outside
stage of San Giovanni during its metamorphosis that
in those days one could not imagine the place without him. He was there always and everywhere: in
winter with beret and wind-cheater, plus-fours, thick
woolen stockings, and mountain boots; in summer
with pith helmet, short-sleeved, open-necked shirt,
and "colonial" pants. He was indeed "a man for all
seasons."

He laid the editorial and administrative foundations for that news sheet which has prospered and
developed into its very fine successor of today. Naturally, here too he needed willing and capable
helpers, and just as naturally, against the San Giovanni background, he found them. I hesitate to
name any names, but it is not possible to speak of
the *Bollettino* and its present-day descendant without paying tribute to its by now long-time editor, Pio
Trombetta. This extremely dedicated man became
its soul.

Dr. Sanguinetti played his great role not only
outside the monastery but within it. He was also "a
man for all seasons" for Padre Pio himself. When he
died so unexpectedly, Douglas Woodruff wrote to
me: "How very strange! One had always imagined
the good Doctor surviving Padre Pio, and growing
old against a background of reminiscent stories
about him." He would certainly have been able to
recount some absorbing ones, for, apart from the
many extraordinary happenings of which he was a
witness, Padre Pio repaid his total attachment by
giving him extreme confidence. With the doctor, as
with his confessor and sometime Superior, Padre
Agostino, he felt no need to maintain his habitual

vigilant defense against the invading curiosity of people, sometimes even of the best-intentioned.

Dr. Sanguinetti did not speak to me a great deal of past events or previous conversations with Padre Pio, for, of course, the incredible saga was in full flow, and astounding happenings, as well as memorable judgments, counsels, or comments, were the order of the day. But some little snippets I do recall. He told me that one day Padre Pio had told him he would not lose one of all those who came to seek his help.

Another day, when the doctor entered his cell, he found him praying. As he finished, he said, "Please excuse me. I was saying some prayers for my grandfather." "But you told me he was already in heaven." "That is so," said Padre Pio, "but the prayers that I have now said and shall yet say for him have helped him to get there."

Simple words; but a most illuminating window on eternity, where past, present, and future have not that consecutive relevance that we know. It was an understanding of this on his part that constituted the chief source and motivation of all Padre Pio's life of suffering.

He was deeply moved and saddened by the thought of Christ's isolation and abandonment during His Passion, till it suddenly came to him that in virtue of what has just been said, by his voluntary participation in Our Lord's sufferings *now* he could be alongside Him and share in them *then*. It was then that he began to seek this participation with all the intensity at his command, requesting that in his purely human measure he be permitted to suffer as much as possible without dying.

The Lord granted him his request. For fifty long years that hourly and daily immolation continued; and it was thus that he was able to obtain for others innumerable graces and favors. Thus also can it be understood that his perpetual self-control, his cheerfulness and good humor, were to say the least of it heroic and of a supernatural nature.

That good humor Dr. Sanguinetti had seen him display in varied and extraordinary circumstances. He came in one terribly hot and stifling day from one of his long spells in the confessional and told him how, feeling absolutely drained of strength, when he looked out at the dense, waiting mass of people through whom he would have to make his way, he felt he just could not manage it. "Then," said he with a chuckle of continuing happy surprise, "you should have seen their faces when they saw me take leave of them from the door on the other side of them!"

But that is another and a bigger story on which I shall shortly enlarge.

Let me give one last reminiscence of Dr. Sanguinetti by telling of his invitation to a geological conference at Foggia. He had no serious intention of going, but happening to be in town that day, and remembering they were going to discuss the results of a survey done on the Gargano Peninsula of which San Giovanni forms part, he thought that, late though it was, he might as well put in an appearance. The proceedings were just drawing to a close, and as one of the promoters greeted him, he apologized, saying, "Sorry not to have made it in time. Was there anything of interest for my neck of the woods?" "Well," said the other, "it has been established beyond any reasonable doubt that the peninsula is going to drop into the sea." "Good God! When?" "The experts think in roughly ten thousand years." "Aha!" said Dr. Sanguinetti. "I'm not going to worry, for I would willingly bet our hospital will have a new administrator by then!"

Since that day there have been several new administrators in the hospital, and in the normal course of events there should be many more. But the bust of Dr. Sanguinetti stands on its pedestal in the wide entrance hall and will stand there sentinel-like as long as the hospital lasts. That, of course, is his outside job. On the inside, as was his wont, he is again and always alongside Padre Pio.

CHAPTER VIII

There used to be a cheerful ditty in the days of my youth called "The Man on the Flying Trapeze." I recall only a couple of lines of the refrain, which ran:

He flies through the air with the greatest of ease,
That daring young man on the flying trapeze! . . .

As we have seen from the confessional story, that young man had nothing on Padre Pio; for no onlooking eye was able even to glimpse the path of his flight. And that is only half the story; never did the young man in question aspire to such agility as to be in two places at the same time—which Padre Pio was eminently capable of.

One of the converted Communists I met at San Giovanni Rotondo said to me: "Since my conversion I have read a great number of lives of saints, to try and discover what is the essential ingredient of sainthood. I have come to the conclusion that a man is the more a saint the more he resembles Christ. And that is what so attracts me to Padre Pio: his immense Christlikeness."

One thing at least is certain. If individual saints have been outstanding for particular saintly characteristics or consequent activities, no one has ever appeared to combine so many or all of them as did

Padre Pio. Seer, prophet, mind reader, miracle worker, confessor extraordinary, missionary—on a world-wide scale—mystic, ascetic: all these things he was to an extraordinary degree. He was also the only priest-stigmatist among the small number of stigmatists the Church has ever been willing to recognize. And to cap it all, he was a bi-locationist.

In the long history of the Church, the saints accredited with serious evidence of bi-location can be counted on one hand—with fingers left over. It is a tremendous reversal of the laws of nature to ask anyone to accept. I am reminded of the answer given by Benedetto Croce, the southern Italian philosopher, when someone asked him if he believed in the Evil Eye. "Of course not!" said Croce. "How could one?—But, mind you," he added, "it exists!" And against all the laws of nature, Padre Pio's bi-location most definitely existed.

At first, in the early days, it was not spoken of a great deal except among his immediate followers. Perhaps the two earliest assertions of it are those saying that he appeared to General Cadorna when he was on the point of committing suicide after the disaster of Caporetto; and that he was seen in St. Peter's at the beatification of the Little Flower. But people tended to dismiss these as pure folklore.

Then the detailed instances of it gradually began to increase, and eventually, as his Superior, Padre Carmelo da Sessano, said to me in a burst of confidence, he was "appearing all over the place!" Equally gradually, more and more people began to discuss it openly and to accept it, again "all over the place."

The occasion of Padre Carmelo's confidence was

a book I had brought down with me. It was a slim volume entitled simply *Padre Pio,* by an Irish author named Malachy Carroll. "Look, Father," I told him, "this is only a booklet, but it is one of the best publications on Padre Pio I have ever seen. No rhetoric, no superstition, everything set down quietly and matter-of-factly, including even his bi-location." The Father Guardian hesitated and then said, "I would not say this to many people, but I am afraid we may even be confronted now not just with *bi*-location but with *multi*-location." He then used the phrase I have quoted, and added, "Even here he has been doing it openly. Right here last week in the village!"

There had been a concert in the hall adjoining the monastery, and Padre Pio had been asked if he would like to join the group of friars who would be there along with the people. He assented willingly and, seated among the group, followed the various items with obvious interest and appreciation. At the interval, however, while the others chatted, he placed his arms on the back of the chair in front of him and rested his head on them, remaining silent and motionless. His companions, thinking he was fatigued, left him undisturbed; and thus he stayed for about five minutes. Then, as the interval was ending, he sat back again and resumed contact with the others. No one thought any more about it.

Early the following day, however, Padre Carmelo went to visit a house where there was a person seriously ill. Not only was the patient in excellent spirits, but he found the whole household jubilant.

It was well known that Padre Pio never left the monastery—normally, that is—except to cast his vote at election time, and latterly for a rare visit to the hospital. The family therefore could hardly contain themselves as they gathered around Padre Carmelo saying how marvelous it was that Padre Pio had come to see them yesterday evening.

The Guardian looked at them in astonishment. "But," he protested, "Padre Pio didn't come into the village yesterday evening." It was their turn to be amazed at his ignorance of the visit. "Yes, yes, Father! Of course he did! He came here to see us last night. Didn't you know?" When he asked them at what time the visit had taken place, he already knew the answer. It was at the time of the concert interval.

Doesn't it sound incredible? But no more so than that God should have marked a priest of obvious deep piety with the open, bleeding wounds of Christ's passion and death; that He should have given him the power to perform the most astounding miracles and to live the life he lived. To my way of thinking, it is much more incredible that the world at large and to a great extent the Church herself should have paid so little attention.

CHAPTER IX

There are many well-authenticated accounts of Padre Pio's appearances in bi-location, and to others of which I have personal knowledge I shall also refer, but the instance of which I should like to speak now is for several reasons my favorite. First of all it happened to a man whom Padre Pio held in great affection; secondly, he was held in similar affection by us all. No one could possibly help liking Giovanni Gigliozzi. And thirdly, the incident ended in a fashion most characteristic of Padre Pio, with just a fatherly smile and a joke.

Giovanni I have not seen for years, and he must now be getting on. But should he live to be a hundred, he will always be one of those beloved of the gods who die young in spirit. Then, however, he was young both in body and in spirit, full of deep interest in life and in people, and a well-known Roman writer and broadcaster. He was also an assiduous disciple of Padre Pio's, and participated enthusiastically in every way he could in the various San Giovanni activities, especially in the *Bollettino*.

It happened that he was at times subject to extremely violent attacks of migraine, for at least one very good reason that I can think of. When he got a good idea for a book or for a newspaper or broadcasting series, he would neglect such things as the passage of time and the necessity for sleep or nourishment. He was liable to keep plugging away for twenty-four hours or more.

His migraines, when they arrived, were terrible, blinding him with pain and making work and rest equally impossible. One day he was hit by one at a most inopportune moment. He was due to broadcast and he could not remotely think of attempting it. The director of his program in Rome's Broadcasting House was aghast. "But, Giovanni, you must!" "I can't! I'm absolutely desperate!" The director, in his own quiet desperation, led him into a room, settled him on a couch "to see if it would pass," as he said, and hurried off to try and arrange some half-reasonable substitution.

Giovanni knew that the attack would not pass for some considerable time, and he lay there writhing in pain, with all his consciousness concentrated on standing up to it. There was no thought of Padre Pio in his mind. Then he seemed to hear a step by the couch and the familiar "click" of a great "pair" of rosary beads. He opened his eyes, and there was Padre Pio looking down at him.

He told me that it was so sudden and completely unexpected that he was frightened out of his wits and let out a yell, so that it was surprising no one came rushing in. I imagine also that he felt it was a sign he was going to die.

Padre Pio spoke no word but gazed at him with his customary smile of affection, laid his hand on his head, and disappeared. So too did the migraine, and Giovanni, when he had regained his composure, went out to the general surprise of all concerned and did his program. Naturally, people were curious and questioned him at the end of it; but all he would say was that fortunately and surprisingly the pain had seemed to go just as suddenly as it had come.

On Sunday he went down to San Giovanni, and when he got there Padre Pio was in the midst of his evening talk with his collaborators. Dropping on one knee, he kissed one of those wounded hands; and as he knelt there, Padre Pio said to him, "Well, Giovanni, and how is the head?" "Thank you, Padre," Giovanni earnestly replied, "very well indeed." "Ah," said Padre Pio, and he smiled as though at a little joke they had in common, "these hallucinations!"

CHAPTER X

"*La bontà che cammina!*" he said. It means
"Goodness walking," and it is not a very poetic
phrase. There was, however, plenty of poetry in the
speaker's tough face, and in his eyes unashamedly
brimming with tears, as we looked after Padre Pio
leaving the sacristy on those suffering, pierced feet.

It was another Giovanni who was speaking. But a
very different one. Giovanni da Prato he was called,
after the name of the town from which he came. I
looked upon him as a brother, and still do, but that
was the only name by which I ever knew him. No
one called him anything else.

His introduction to Padre Pio had been rather
different from most. It might fairly be described as
dramatic.

He was a taxi driver, a violent Communist, and
when he got drunk he was very liable to beat up his
wife. One night he had done just that; and then,
staggering into their bedroom, he had flung himself
on the bed.

At that moment he felt the bed being heavily
shaken from the lower bedrail and, looking down, to
his amazement he saw a Capuchin friar grasping the
rail and gazing at him angrily. The friar told him in
no uncertain terms what he thought of him and his
conduct, and then he seemed to be no longer there.

Giovanni leaped from the bed, ran quickly and

locked the front door, and then, going into the kitchen, shouted to his wife: "Now then, where's that so-and-so monk?"

Brushing aside her protests and denials, he searched the house thoroughly, found no one, and by that time was sober enough to be convinced by his wife's sincerity.

She, poor woman, when she heard his story felt at once that there was only one explanation, but she could hardly credit it. She had long been praying for Padre Pio's help, and she had heard of his powers of bi-location; but was it possible that he had given her this tremendous answer and come here personally to her home? What other explanation could there be?

"It was Padre Pio!" she exclaimed, and in her exultation her husband's puzzled curses and imprecations ran off her like water.

Giovanni, however, was made of stern stuff. "Look," he said, "no monk makes a monkey out of me. I'm going down to have a look at this Padre Pio of yours and hear what he has to say for himself. I'll also find out if he flies!"

Some days later, good as his word, he got into his taxi and grimly made the long trip from Tuscany down to the Gargano Peninsula. He found Padre Pio, recognized him, and spoke to him. Like the rest of us, he was thunder-struck; and Padre Pio led him like a lamb to the confessional.

Giovanni, who was generally not much troubled by human respect, had no difficulty in giving me an account of what took place there.

"What I forgot," he said, "he recalled for me. I was weeping, and he was weeping too." At the end, when he pulled out his Communist Party membership card and asked Padre Pio to destroy it, he got the reply "Yes, I shall. But you have another of these cards in the drawer by the head of your bed. Destroy that too when you go home."

The penitent, more than ever impressed, was psychologically put to rights, comforted and consoled, and Padre Pio promised to stay alongside him and to assist him. But now, before the act of contrition and the absolution, came the payoff.

"You have given great scandal," said Padre Pio, "and now you must do something to make up for it. For your penance you will go every Sunday to Holy Communion at last Mass in the main church until I tell you to stop."

In those days there were no such things as relaxed fasting rules or evening Masses, and those going to Communion did so before partaking of breakfast, and therefore at one of the earlier Masses. Absolutely no one ever went to Communion at the last, or midday, Mass. But each Sunday the unhappy Giovanni had to march down the aisle, to the amazement and whispered comments of the congregation; and, until it became recognized as a fixture the attention of the celebrating priest had regularly to be drawn to the solitary figure kneeling at the sanctuary rails. "I lost kilograms in sweat," said Giovanni.

This penance lasted for the better part of a year; but during his many visits in the course of it he never asked to be let off. On the other hand, he did something else.

He had been an outstanding figure among his Communist companions. Now he had become a regular "Holy Joe." However, precisely because he was the man he was, and still possessed a ready fist, few were those who ventured any humorous observations, and even then only in a very friendly fashion.

For those who did make such comment or remonstrance on his changed outlook, Giovanni had a ready answer. "Right! Why don't you come down with me and see how *you* make out?" A cheap trip to the south in such colorful company was attractive, and naturally there was also a great curiosity. And so it came to pass that month after month he would arrive with a cargo of Reds. Always they were impressed, and often they were converted; and for some time Giovanni's squads became a regular feature at San Giovanni Rotondo. I remember seeing him march off one of his cohorts to the hospital, where they were looking for blood donors. "Boys," he was saying, "they need blood and we've got loads of it. Come on!"

One evening he came over to me with a casual air and asked me, surprisingly, "How much courage have you got?" "As much as the next." "Good," said he with a grin, "will you accompany me on a perilous piece of exploration?"

Padre Pio had been ill and was confined to his cell. The bar was up and no lay visitors were being admitted to the monastery. Giovanni produced a key. "This," said he, "is a key I had cut from one I just happened to come by. It opens the door that leads in from the sacristy. Is anyone going to prevent us from seeing and paying our respects to our beloved Padre?"

He opened the door softly and let it stand ajar for a moment. Then he said, "Now, you see, if anyone questions us we can say that the door was standing

open. It is, isn't it?" (Scripture tells us, "Be ye as
cunning as serpents.") We further enacted the scrip-
tural injunction by proceeding as gently as doves to
the cell; and here Padre Pio reproached us not at all
but gave us his blessing and an affectionate thump
on the head with his mittened hand.

No man questioned or condemned us; and as we
came out, with Giovanni smiling in triumph, I felt,
not for the first time, that Jesuits and Communists
had a great deal of technical ground in common.

CHAPTER XI

Many other tales of Padre Pio's bi-locationary feats I should like to tell, tales which were common knowledge at San Giovanni. I always liked very much that of the man who was a frequent visitor and who during a long car run fell asleep at the wheel. He woke up some minutes later and, looking at the surrounding countryside, found that for quite a distance the car had been doing very nicely on its own. When he next came down, he was read a semi-serious lecture by Padre Pio on the hardships of one's being hauled out car driving at short notice!

However, I intend to narrate only those tales with whose participants I had some kind of personal contact or link, direct or indirect; because I realize that otherwise many readers might justifiably think such narratives to be the product of credulity or wishful thinking on my part, and of popular fantasy. They would be wrong, because there are few greater skeptics than the present writer, but they cannot know that.

The following story begins with an illustration of such skepticism. Despite all the wonders I had witnessed and experienced, when it was recounted to me that during the last war Padre Pio had appeared in the sky above San Giovanni and turned back an American bombing mission, I considered it another good Mediterranean myth and dismissed it, until I met Douglas Woodruff in a Rome hotel during one of his trips. He told me of the experience his friend Lord Eldon had had during the previous week. He had met casually on the Foggia train the American squadron leader chiefly concerned. That would seem direct enough contact to justify my telling this tale too.

An American bombing mission was nearing its target close to Foggia when the squadron leader saw something absolutely unbelievable in front of his plane. It was the figure of a monk holding up his hands in the gesture of turning him back. He did what most of us would undoubtedly have done in the circumstances—turned back. However, when, having jettisoned the bombs in open country, or chosen another target, he arrived back at base and told his story, his C.O. also did what most of us would have done—ordered him to hospital for observation.

Bombing-mission fatigue was a familiar enough phenomenon—even though it had never before been known to take this peculiar form of spotting monks in the clouds—and after rest and whatever seemed the best initial treatment, he would be sent back to the States on special medical leave.

Now the squadron leader was as astonished and bewildered as anybody, for while he felt completely normal and rational, he yet realized that his vision or his imagination must have played him a devastating trick. But his worries were considerably lightened when an Italian orderly who had heard the gossip came quietly to him one day and suggested that perhaps he had not been deceived as everyone thought, because in that region there lived a monk

said to have the most miraculous powers, and he
personally had no difficulty in accepting that what
he had seen had been there for him to see.

This was a life line, and the squadron leader so
held onto it that, after the war and a number of
inquiries, he arrived at San Giovanni to check. In
Padre Pio he recognized his quondam acquaintance
of the skies and had the veracity of the encounter
admitted to him. And when Lord Eldon met him on
the train, he and his wife were returning to visit an
old friend.

CHAPTER XII

The next bi-locationary tale was related to me by Father Dominic in his cell.

It is a tale within a tale, and we shall start with the one which provided the occasion for the other.

Monsignor Damiani, Vicar-General of the diocese of Salto in Uruguay, had great belief in Padre Pio and had come to visit him. In view of his ecclesiastical standing, he was able to stay in the monastery itself. He had a weak heart, and one day when Padre Pio was confessing his usual large number of penitents in church, he had an attack. He begged those tending him to inform Padre Pio at once. This was done urgently, but without effect. Padre Pio quietly acknowledged the message and went on confessing.

When he came to the monsignor's bedside, considerable time had passed and the attack was over. The sick man reproached him for not coming when he had called for him, but Padre Pio told him in the most natural way that he knew it had not been necessary, because the attack was not fatal. "Ah, how I wish that I could remain here and be assisted by you on my deathbed," said the monsignor. "Do not worry," was the response, "I shall assist you wherever you are."

The Vicar-General returned to his diocese, and

naturally he recounted this episode to his bishop and his intimates. They knew, therefore, what he was talking about when one morning he was found dying and on his bedside table there lay a scrawled message of three words. It said: "Padre Pio came."

The news of this, of course, caused much talk among the friars at San Giovanni, and it was one of the extraordinary happenings that Father Dominic recounted to his father when he was visiting him in Milwaukee. The old man was quiet for some time, and then he said, "Son, you know him well. You are his friend. Will you ask him to help me here when *my* time comes?" Father Dominic felt he had to promise.

He then told me how awkward and embarrassed he felt after his return at having to make such a request. But a father was a father, and a promise was a promise; and the first time he was alone with Padre Pio he explained, apologized, and made the request. Padre Pio, he said, gave him an understanding look, spoke no word, but slowly nodded.

Two years later Father Dominic was in the process of setting off for home again when he received a cable that his father was dead. By the time he got there, he was buried.

He had died in the house of a married daughter; and when Father Dominic inquired of his sister what were the circumstances of his death, this, briefly, is what she told him.

Her husband and she, when the weather was good, were accustomed to help her father out during the afternoon and leave him comfortably seated on a veranda where he might enjoy some sunshine. He was unable to move around by himself, and so they could not believe their eyes when on this particular day they went to bring him back to his room and found him no longer there. Not a step had been heard, nor a door opening or closing.

They hurried to his bedroom and, sure enough, there he was, lying in bed, eyes closed, mouth slightly open, "And, Dominic," said his sister, "we saw a Host on his tongue!"

CHAPTER XIII

Here is a story from nearer home, from the town of Donegal where, until his death some dozen years ago, one of its most jovial and best-known characters was a man called Christy Gallagher.

Christy dealt in eggs and poultry in quite a large way, and to all and sundry he was known as "Christy Egg." He was larger than life both in his outlook and in his colorful conversation. I could have listened to him for hours.

His holidays were mostly jaunts to the big English race meetings at Epsom or Ascot or Newmarket; and on his return one would receive a vivid account of whom or what he had observed, sometimes in the Royal Enclosure! He was a county councilor of long standing, and he was known and liked all over the county and indeed in much of the country.

He was a large man physically, had boxed in his youth, and still seemed chock full of vitality. It was therefore a shattering piece of news when we heard that he too had fallen victim to the great killer disease of our times.

He took it like the man he was, putting up a gallant fight and bracing himself for defeat if it came.

Christy had great admiration for Padre Pio; and when my wife told his wife she would, if he so desired, send him a piece of bandage which had bound the wound on one of Padre Pio's hands, he was delighted. We sent it to the Dublin hospital where by then he was and told him to keep it as long as he liked.

Every so often we had news of him, and it was always the same. Christy was as cheerful as ever and continuing to use the ring as best he could. However, eventually the bell went for the last round and we heard that he had gone—but, as I learned later, against what a large-scale, lightsome Christy background!

When his wife went to see him one day, she found him brimming over with high spirits. "Do you know what happened during the night?" he asked her. "Padre Pio came here, spoke to me, and asked me whether I would like to have Communion!" After getting over his initial shock, he had said, "Yes, I would," and had received Holy Communion. But as Padre Pio was going, Christy, thanking him, gave the measure of his ebullient personality. "Father," said he, "there is another Donegal man in a ward along the corridor, and I know he would like to see you too!"

Christy was really jubilant that morning. He thought the visit was a marvelous sign that he was going to be all right. He was quite correct; but not as he had read it.

The date was September 23, 1968; and later in the day he was thunder-struck to hear over his radio the announcement of Padre Pio's death. Some short time later Christy unexpectedly, quietly and peacefully, thoroughly prepared, was just no longer there one morning.

This tale needs a comment. The Irish are not clannish as are the Scots. They say that "a Scotsman loves his brother Scot, but an Irishman loves his native land." An Irishman's admiration for the emergence of one of his fellow countrymen above the ranks of his peers tends to be rather restrained; and this tendency is no whit abated at local level.

Consequently, I can well imagine that many residents of Donegal town, while perfectly willing to accept it for the unknown inhabitant of some remoter region, would very readily scoff at the idea of anything so blatantly preternatural happening to their townsman Christy Egg. "What?" they would say. "A thing like that happen to old Christy? Not on your life! Christy dreamed it all!"

They may be right. Who is to say? But, if they are, wasn't it a grand and comforting dream to have?

The memory of it has been of great consolation to his wonderful wife and his children; all the more so since, being aware of the down-to-earth realism that underlay Christy's jocularity and bonhomie, they, like my own wife and myself, have little doubt about the true nature of his experience.

CHAPTER XIV

I mentioned sending off a piece of bloodstained bandage that had bound one of Padre Pio's hands; and I know that this would be considered by many people as "mumbo-jumbo." But is it?

Such people are possibly blind to the miracles of the everyday world surrounding them; things like their sight itself, their hearing, the circulation of their blood, not to mention the trees and grass, the seasons and, in general, the order of the universe. If they are Christians, they perhaps forget a phrase in the Gospels, the second half of which I have already quoted: "They sought to touch His garment; for virtue went out from Him."

At San Giovanni people certainly thought that virtue went out from Padre Pio; and not only would they seek to touch his garment, but they were not above trying surreptitiously to snip off the end of his white, knotted Franciscan girdle!

This belief may tend at times to superstition, but there is nothing fundamentally unreasonable about it.

An old church will take on, not just a patina of time, but an aura of sanctity predisposing one to prayer; the possessions of those dear to us acquire some participation in their personality. As we are creatures whose emotions and thoughts are activated through the senses, physical objects have the power to sharpen and condition our feelings and reactions.

Whether there is more to it than that, whether physical objects can become objective vehicles for the transmission of spiritual or physical benefits, is a deeper question: "There are more things in heaven and earth, Horatio . . .", and I firmly believe they can. So too, clearly, does the Church, as is evidenced not only by her agelong custom of preserving and distributing the relics of saints, but also by her blessing of things such as holy water, the holy oils, etc.

At any rate, seldom did anyone go to San Giovanni Rotondo without bringing away for relatives and friends some medals or other religious objects which Padre Pio had blessed.

Naturally, if one could get hold of something which had been directly associated with Padre Pio, this was a prized possession. Many were the innocent subterfuges used. People would present him with a new pair of brown mittens specially knitted for him, and would hope to get the pair he was wearing in exchange! Sometimes, if they were lucky, they did.

My own treasured piece of bandage came to me through the adventurous subterfuge of a friar of San Giovanni and the generosity of that great Dublin Capuchin, Father Senan, the man under whose brilliant and humorous editorship the Irish *Capuchin Annual* became famous.

Father Senan was outraged when he heard that one who had had so much contact with Padre Pio did not possess a piece of the bandages which bound his wounds. "Impossible!" he exclaimed. "We cannot have it!" And taking his own piece of bloodstained bandage, he cut it in two and gave me half.

"How did you come by it?" I asked him. "Well," said Father Senan, with his characteristic twinkle, "actually it was stolen!"

The fact was that, having asked one of the friars of San Giovanni, whom he had met in Rome, whether he could oblige him with some object associated with Padre Pio, this victim of the Senan blarney hit upon the idea of asking Padre Pio whether he could fetch water up to his cell for him when he was carrying up some for himself. Padre Pio thanked him; and the good friar, having looked around, purloined some bandage that he found there. Pondering afterward the ease of the operation, he made bold to repeat the offer the following evening, with some other friend in mind. Padre Pio gave him an old-fashioned look and replied, "No, no, dear Father! Please don't trouble. I have a great aversion to having *thieves* in my cell!" But he did not demand return of the spoils, and so, I suppose, Father Senan turned me into a fellow accessory after the crime.

I have still, as well as the bandage, an ever decreasing store of medals blessed by him, as well as some clippings from his tonsure trimming! But, above all, my wife and I have little "holy pictures" with a prayer which he wrote on them for each of us. These are our most prized possessions.

CHAPTER XV

I have also some photographs, greatly cherished, taken in company with Padre Pio. These are due to the kindness of Padre Giacomo, who became semi-official photographer in the monastery and supplied the *Bollettino* and subsequent magazine with some of its loveliest illustrations.

Padre Pio cared not at all for being photographed or filmed, but he accepted it when he could not avoid it, with as good grace as he could muster, or even willingly if he thought the circumstances justified it. Padre Giacomo learned to become very adept at snapping him unobtrusively; but I possess one photograph in which the expression on his face as he sees the camera about to click shows clearly that he thinks the thing is being overdone.

And apropos of that, perhaps I might tell of some souvenir photographs that just never happened.

It was during the summer months, and because of the crowds and the heat Padre Pio was saying Mass under a portico adjacent to the old church, while the congregation stood in the *piazza*. It was one of the seven occasions on which I had the privilege of serving his Mass, and my old and energetic friend, Gino Ghisleri, had determined that this one had to be preserved for posterity. He got hold of a local professional photographer and enjoined him to do a good job. This he told me after Mass, and said that the photographs were to be ready by four o'clock in the afternoon.

I went with him to collect them, and I must confess to having been very eager to see what the photographer had produced. He was not there; but his sister was, and she informed an irate and incredulous Gino that there was nothing to collect.

This was one of the times when San Giovanni reminded me of the *Fioretti* of St. Francis. Their innocence and legendary atmosphere appeared in the absolute naturalness with which the girl responded to the Ghisleri onslaught. "No, *signore*," she said in calm explanation. "There is nothing to be done about it. My brother, you see, tried to be too smart." "What do you mean, 'too smart'?" snorted Gino. "Well, as Padre Pio was coming around to the altar," she replied, "he saw my brother with his camera and said to him that he must take no more than one or two photographs during the Mass. My brother agreed, but then shot two whole rolls. They all came out blank." She looked at us as who should say, "What else could you expect? How could anyone be so foolish?"

I told the story that evening to Dr. Sanguinetti, who said, "No! Don't tell me! Do you realize that exactly the same thing happened to me? Two rolls and all!"

The roof of the hospital had just been completed and there was already a lift, so the doctor and his colleagues were most anxious that Padre Pio should come across from the monastery and stand upon the vast, flat top of the structure now finished in its essentials. He accepted, and a party of friars and laymen were on the roof to welcome him. As he walked around complimenting those responsible, and agreeing with those enthusing over the splendid panoramas, the doctor thought this an excellent occasion to get some pictures. He took his first snap as Padre Pio was turning away from his first look over the parapet, and just at that moment a gust of wind blew the heavy scarf he was wearing across his face. When he readjusted it and saw the camera he called, "No, *Dottore;* no photographs, please!" "Right, Padre," assented Dr. Sanguinetti, "Sorry!" And then, moving around in the background, he continued to take one quiet photograph after another, on the roof and on the way back to the monastery, until he had used up the two rolls spoken of. They all came out blank, except the first one with the scarf blowing across Padre Pio's face, the one he had shot before being forbidden!

I must add a postscript concerning, not a photograph, but a painting.

Among those who had come to live permanently at San Giovanni were Count Telfner and his wife. The count himself had always been greatly attracted by things ecclesiastical; they had begun their married life in Assisi; and his wife told me that she had become very bored by the fact that their guests were almost invariably priests and friars. It came as a great relief when her husband decided to move to that other piece of Umbrian paradise, Perugia.

"But," she related, "picture my feelings when, wishing to make a telephone call before our line had been connected, I went to the neighboring house to telephone, and almost the first thing that met my eye was a great austere painting of a friar!"

After her phone call, however, she had a closer

look at the picture; and the laughter she indulged in was the first step toward journey's end for her husband and herself. (They have been in San Giovanni now for half a lifetime and, I imagine, will never leave it.) For the painting had something written on it.

The owner of the house was the artist. He was a man of stern temperament; and when he decided to do a portrait of Padre Pio, perhaps unconsciously he invested the face with his own severity. Whether or not, the portrait that emerged was a truly daunting one.

Before hanging it up, he took it down to San Giovanni to show it to Padre Pio and ask him to bestow a blessing upon it for the household. At the same time he asked him if he would be so kind as to write some message upon it. "Ah, yes," said Padre Pio, looking at the picture with a peculiar expression, "I shall certainly do that."

The message he wrote was the one that sparked off the change in the countess' entire life. It was a very simple one. All it said was: "Don't be afraid. It's only me!"

CHAPTER XVI

In the previous chapter there strode onto the stage (the only way Gino would ever make his appearance) Gino Ghisleri, another highly important person in the world of San Giovanni, no less a man than the successor of Dr. Sanguinetti.

I had met him at the home of one of Milan's younger industrialists. In the drawing room after dinner, because of something that was said, I decided to shock my fellow guests by casually introducing the subject of Padre Pio and then letting them have both barrels. The effect was devastating, and Gino Ghisleri and his son, who were sincere and practicing Catholics, were among those who approached me privately afterward and wanted to know more. We became fast friends and we went down to San Giovanni several times together.

When the bombshell of Dr. Sanguinetti's death took place and I arrived back at the end of the summer, the main structure of the hospital had been finished, but there was still a vast amount of interior and infrastructural work to be done; then it had to be furnished, technically equipped, departmentally organized and staffed, and set going. It was a herculean task, and the great trouble was that a large number of people mistakenly thought they were capable of handling it.

Occasions such as this were very difficult for

Padre Pio. Each person he knew was a soul to be saved, for each he was a father, an individual father. How could he hurt them by telling them bluntly they were not up to it?

He was good enough to confide in me, and one day I said to him, "Padre, I know many constructional engineers who are not saints, and a number of saints who are not constructional engineers. But I know one man who is an extremely good engineer and who has also a very sound religious outlook. Furthermore he is as tough as they make them, he has great organizational experience, and he has been down here with me several times. Would you like to see him?"

It was not difficult to persuade Gino to take a weekend off and come down to San Giovanni. On the way I dwelt at great length on the tremendous extra burdens that Dr. Sanguinetti's death had thrown on Padre Pio, and on the extreme difficulty of finding an adequate successor. At length he was moved to say that he wished *he* could do something. He meant it, for under his toughness, and with all his competence, he had a deep fundamental humility, and he really thought that he would be far from adequate. I explained to him that this was not the case and arrived at the monastery with a willing candidate.

Gino Ghisleri had fought in the First World War as a very young volunteer who had falsified his age in order to get into the army. After the war, as an engineering student, he had organized opposition to the rising wave of Communism and had been wounded in a pitched armed battle in Milan's Cathedral Square. He was also a member of a flying column of young men who could be called into action anywhere a religious procession was liable to be attacked. (Their technique was to carry staves painted white to look like great candles, with bits of real lighted candles stuck into their tops!)

During the inter-war years he performed famous feats of engineering. Roads, tunnels, aqueducts, dams from the Alps to Sicily and in the former Italian territories of Africa carry his signature. His too was the initial stretch of the famous *Autostrada del Sole,* his the first sector of Milan's underground railway, after the Second World War was over. And during that war he had played a not inconsiderable part in the Italian resistance movement.

Such was the man I brought down with me to carry on where my other old friend had left off. And Padre Pio, after he had spoken to him at length in his cell, said with satisfaction, "Yes, this is the man. He has a great and good heart. And I have told him I am willing to make of him the sacrifice that at God's request Abraham was ready to make of Isaac!" He did not have to. Gino almost brought that sacrifice upon himself.

There had been only one doubt in my mind at the time. While his capacity and dynamism were unquestionable, would he, could he devote the necessary time away from his other activities? I need not have worried. He it was who worried himself sick, not over those other activities, but over whether he was letting Padre Pio down.

He was so made, however, as not to want to abandon any of his manifold works, but just to expand his efforts. All the pleas of his family, of myself, and even of Padre Pio were of no avail. Time and again he seemed to be on the verge of collapse, but always he dredged up the necessary strength, till eventually Padre Pio told him he had as much margin left as would "cover a parsley leaf," and ordered him off for rest. But by then his task was done, the hospital had been opened, and the great project passed to him by Dr. Sanguinetti was in full swing.

So too still, I am happy to say, is Gino Ghisleri.

CHAPTER XVII

If one thinks just for a moment of what is implied in the setting up of a modern four-hundred-bed hospital, the immensity and complexity of the task are evident. Situate it then in the middle of nowhere; make all its prodigious running costs depend upon more or less haphazard charitable donations; consider that it was so constructed as to be capable of harmonious expansion to its present number of a thousand beds. And then ask what force created it.

No amount of thought and planning (for where were the stable elements?) or even of human blood, sweat, and tears ever produced that vast and continuing phenomenon. It took a vision not of this world to foresee it all, and a powerhouse of prayer and suffering to bring it to fruition.

But it needed human collaboration too, and it got it from the devoted band of Padre Pio's disciples, chief among them the man just described in the last chapter.

Before the great day of the hospital's inauguration, Gino Ghisleri came the nearest he possibly could to a bi-location of his own! Along with his constructional labors, he scoured Italy for the right type of doctors and surgeons, medical consultants, nurses, and for a body of experienced nursing nuns who would be both launchers and leavens. It was extremely difficult to find these last, because all the best ones were already fully committed: but there was great good will. I remember visiting a well-known Milan clinic with him and hearing a very tired-looking nun who was in charge say with all the earnestness in the world but with no hope: "Just imagine if I should not love to work in Padre Pio's hospital. I try to accompany him in prayer every morning at the time of his Holy Mass!"

But Gino eventually found suitable sisters; and a great and wonderful job they have done, these nuns, by their dedication and expertise, and by the way they have trained, spiritually and professionally, the continuous intake of student nurses for such an extraordinary institution.

The medical recruitment would obviously have been beyond his powers had he not had expert advice and assistance. This he received in abundant measure from Professor Pietro Valdoni, one of Italy's most brilliant surgeons, and a man of great refinement and charm. He it was who was responsible not only for finding the right incumbents for the key posts, but for attracting the right cadres of junior doctors. His reputation and his personal invitations made the cardiological conference which accompanied the inauguration of the hospital an international event. And as the hospital got under way, month after month he came down from Rome to keep a friendly, tactful eye on things and to operate for days on end with no thought of fee or expense.

Eventually Gino's highly intelligent young doctor son-in-law came down with his family to San Giovanni, and in time became Padre Pio's personal physician. With his dash and *panache* he was also for many years the popular mayor of the town.

But all that was in the future. At the moment the eagerly awaited day of the hospital's opening had arrived, a fittingly glorious day of bright sunshine. The official ceremony was performed by Cardinal Lercaro, flown down in an Air Force plane to the Foggia airfield by courtesy of the Italian government. The government itself was represented by another old friend of resistance days, Cesare Merzagora, then president of the Senate. Fifteen thousand people, including hundreds of priests and quite a few bishops, crowded the *piazza*, the road, and the wide space before the hospital entrance. And in the portico topping the steps leading up to the entrance an altar had been erected.

It was here that Padre Pio said the immensely moving inaugural Mass. He was deathly pale, and undoubtedly even more moved than his congregation were. Thousands of people received Communion from a team of surpliced friars and priests. Cardinal Lercaro spoke, but only briefly, saying, "I know that it is not me you want to hear." Padre Pio then addressed us over the microphone, and before the end of that humble, paternal, cleansing homily I doubt if there were many dry eyes among his audience.

In that audience were a number of men whose fame was world-wide, for it had been decided to mark the opening with the international cardiological conference referred to, and the world's greatest heart specialists were there: Paul Dudley White, Eisenhower's specialist, from the States; Evans from London; Olivekronen from Sweden; and so on.

They were fascinated not so much by the conference as by its setting and by the principal personage behind it.

Padre Pio was to receive them on Sunday before lunch, in the largest room available in the monastery, and address them there. It was not very large and made quite a tight squeeze for the group; but, anxious to hear Padre Pio speak, I could not resist slipping in and standing at the rear wall. He made a courteous, almost shy speech of thanks for their kindness in coming there, congratulated them on the dedication of their lives, and gently reminded them of how they could and should tend men's souls as well as their bodies.

Paul Dudley White, a most amiable character, was obviously carried away by Padre Pio himself and all he had witnessed around him. With amazing *gaucherie* that only his emotion could excuse, he kept taking photographs of him, bang up against him, as he spoke; and on leaving, he stammered as a parting salutation, "And, Father—congratulations on your wounds!" Later however, in Rome, I heard him urge Pius XII with much calmer cogency to see in San Giovanni a possible world center for psychosomatic research.

The specialists, on their way out, filed past Padre Pio to be greeted and thanked individually by him; and the Marchese Patrizi, a gifted linguist, said who each was, whence he came, and acted as interpreter in any ensuing conversation. Thus, alas, was my presumptuous little piece of gate crashing discovered, for eventually it was I who arrived before Padre Pio to be "introduced." "Ha!" said he. "And which part of the world, may I ask, do *you* come from?" "A little-known spot, Padre," I replied, "called San Giovanni Rotondo!"—and escaped under the subsequent laughter. But that afternoon in the monastery courtyard he warned my wife, with mock gravity, to keep an eye on her untrustworthy husband. "This morning," said he, "he even disclaimed his native land!"

That night conference and committee members set off for Rome, where we were received next day in special audience by the Pope. He mingled informally with the party for some time, and here the introductions were effected by the committee chairman, that other marchese of ancient lineage, Giovanni Sachetti; for he was not only a good friend of the Holy Father's but by hereditary right one of the leading members of the papal household. Pius XII then addressed us in a characteristic speech in which one did not know what to admire most: his kindheartedness, his intelligence, or his obvious underlying asceticism. What emerged most clearly, however, was his deep respect for the humble servant of God who was the occasion of our presence there that day.

What a tremendous vindication it was for Padre Pio! What a transformation from the days when by order of the Vatican he had been viewed with the deepest suspicion, humiliatingly investigated, and cut off from all contact with the faithful.

But, sad to say, this was no Easter glory. It was to resemble much more the ephemeral triumph of Palm Sunday. And Padre Pio had much of his Master's road to Calvary still to follow, as we shall see.

CHAPTER XVIII

With the advent of the hospital, San Giovanni took on another dimension. New houses for doctors and staff sprang up. Visitors streamed in to see the patients, and they had to find food and accommodation. The hospital had helped to spread the fame of Padre Pio up and down Italy and across the world, and pilgrims began to arrive in ever increasing numbers. Shops, hotels, and guesthouses mushroomed; and adequate parking space had to be provided for the mass of cars and buses that began to converge upon the place.

A great new church had to be built. The monastery was extended and, within limits, given a modern functionality to meet the numerous and varied demands now made upon it. One thinks, for instance, of the vast amount of correspondence that began to pour in from all parts, even from behind the Iron Curtain. This correspondence had to be sorted out and, when it was not in Italian, had to be handled by people conversant at least with the main Western languages. Replies had to be sent.

It was a far cry from the little center of pilgrimage it had been. And yet an amazing thing happened. It was never overrun by commerciality, bureaucracy, or anonymity. And as the hospital and the village seemed to absorb very naturally all human and vehicular traffic respectively, so did the

spirit of St. Francis and his great son appear to contain and vanquish those modern molochs I have
mentioned. San Giovanni Rotondo retained its atmosphere of the *Fioretti* without any seeming effort.

People generally arrived predisposed to good, and
with a common spiritual denominator uniting them.
It was rather like the primitive penitential pilgrimage
of Lough Derg in Donegal, whose original spirit has
likewise survived modernization. To be there implied
of itself a renunciation of worldly values, and the
bare feet, vigil, and fasting of Lough Derg found
their counterpart in the griefs and problems, their
own or of others, that people so often brought along
with them here.

In a word, the magnet, the attraction, remained
the same. Nothing altered fundamentally. Only the
numbers and the dimension changed.

CHAPTER XIX

Earlier on I said that each person had to find his or her own San Giovanni. That was true, psychologically and interpretatively. But there was a broadly common pattern of events and behavior, and if I recount my own experiences, they will serve very well to give the picture.

San Giovanni began when you set out on your journey, for already you had begun to see things in a different perspective and to project yourself toward the great spiritual experience that awaited you. With arrival at Foggia you had the sensation of crossing a physical Rubicon and entering Padre Pio's territorial realm.

(This would probably surprise many burghers of Foggia, who never thought of it. But the visitor struck dumb by the beauty of Venice will find himself alongside a Venetian thinking only of his lunch or his next appointment; and both truth and beauty need the seeing eye.)

As the car sped up toward the red hills, the landmarks with which one became familiar spelled out the approach, and eventually one topped a rise, rounded a bend, and saw the cluster of houses, the road up to the monastery, the monastery itself, and latterly the great hospital. It was a very special moment. Up there was the greatest man in the world today, one of the most sublime saints the world had ever seen—aware of my arrival, as he was, I am convinced, of that of every single soul who came to see him there.

I would install myself at the Hotel Santa Maria delle Grazie, where Mr. and Mrs. Bevilacqua, the hotel proprietors, were the first people who had had the faith, hope, and charity, as well as the means, to build a decent, dignified hotel at San Giovanni. They gave it no undue luxury, as befitted a place of pilgrimage, but it had spacious public rooms, central heating, and running water in the bedrooms (a tremendous innovation when it happened). Many a time I blessed them around four o'clock of a winter's morning for a hot and cold shower before facing up the hill to Mass.

The first evening meal in the dining room was always most interesting. One studied the persons or groups at the small tables, noted or deduced their nationality, wondered about their backgrounds and for what particular reason they had come. Sometimes, alas, by the presence of a cripple, or of a retarded child, it was evident.

After dinner one might drop into a chair at the large log fire in a corner of the lounge. There were very many fascinating people to be met at that fire.

A woman from the Argentine said she had come all that way, not to ask Padre Pio for any favor, but to thank him for a very great one she had already received.

Then there was one of several Italian ex-Communists I met there. Padre Pio, amazingly, had appeared to him and told him to come down here when he was in the act of committing suicide and taking his little daughter with him. He recounted his life story to Piero Pellizzari and myself, and he had been reared in such a deliberately anti-Christian atmosphere that his ignorance of the most fundamental Christian principles was phenomenal.

Piero went out for a stroll with him before turning in, but they were so engrossed in each other's conversation, the one in the pagan innocence of his companion, and the other in the wonders of the new world he had entered, that they decided not to go to bed at all but to continue walking and talking under the quiet stars until it was time for Padre Pio's Mass. As the first figures began to appear through the darkness at that early hour, this newborn disciple marveled at them and exclaimed: "It is incredible! They would not do it for Togliatti!"

By half past ten in the evening at the latest, save perhaps for a quiet group around the lounge fire, the hotel was sunk in silence. Four o'clock came early; and that was when the buzzers generally began to be heard. As long as I live, I shall never forget that characteristic San Giovanni sound: the muffled buzzing of the telephones in room after room as people were roused, and we all soberly realized to what we were being called.

Whether it was the small old church or the large new one, it was always the same. Long before the doors had opened, before the generality of people began to arrive, there was always a waiting group which had begun to form hours before. They had embarked upon their vigil in order to get as close to the altar as possible during the Mass.

The entry of the crowd into the church was accompanied by a rising murmur of sound: typical, vibrant southern Italian voices that sometimes had to be sternly stilled before another ripple of sound, pleased and affectionate, greeted the appearance of Padre Pio and those who were to serve his Mass.

As I have said, I had the unforgettable experience of serving that Mass no less than seven times, and saw his wounded hands close up, without their humble mittens. Later in the book I shall reproduce a short account of the Mass said in the old church, but I should just like to say here one fundamental thing, namely, that as one arrived at and experienced the Consecration, in the midst of a throng of worshipers now deadly silent and at the height of their concentration, one felt that truly this was the center of the universe. Wherever the sacrifice of the Mass is offered up, that is it. But here one realized it.

Here, however, there was also something else. Seldom before in the whole of history, I should think, had that sacrifice been accompanied by such complete awareness of its immensity, and with such utter concomitant self-immolation on the part of the priest. And we were present at that moment in history, here on a remote, barren hillside, in a congregation largely made up of poor people, ignorant in the eyes of the world.

The Mass was in Latin, in that liturgical Latin as old and universal as the Church herself, so that everyone felt at home, both Italians and foreigners; and it was followed by all with a devotion and intensity which, despite any crowding or discomfort there was, made its duration of roughly an hour and a half seem nothing.

Padre Pio did not distribute Holy Communion during Mass excepting when some local child or one brought there specially was making his or her first

Communion. On such occasions, he would give Communion also to the parents and close relatives, inside the sanctuary, on the altar steps.

At the end of Mass, when he made his way to the sacristy, all those male members of the congregation familiar with the routine would follow him there and stand silently while he removed his vestments and then made his first thanksgiving, with head bowed, at a *prie-dieu*. There was complete silence and lack of movement among the men until he had finished.

Afterward, when he arose, a laneway would be made for him to pass along into the monastery; but before he began his slow journey he would bless any objects which people had with them for this purpose. Then, as he moved along, people would kneel for a particular blessing, or to make some request, or just to seek to kiss one of his hands or his garment. At the end, before going on to hear the Mass of his second thanksgiving in the monastery oratory, he would turn, give a last general blessing, and wish everyone *"Buona giornata!"* To this the response would be a great chorus of "To you too, Father!"

The day might now be said to have ended, in its essence, before it really began, because for everyone the Mass was its peak point.

But there were other programs to be projected or attempted, and high on most people's lists was going to confession to Padre Pio. One had to get one's name down and wait one's turn. This, unless for those with foreign passports showing they had come a considerable distance, could mean waiting for anything from one or two days to a week.

Your name being down, it was then essential to see how the numbered list was progressing, so that when your turn approached you would be present among the batch of people waiting, and not be so unfortunate as to miss it. This would never happen, since people would rather sit or stand through several sessions than take any risk.

In any case everyone wanted to be in the church just to be near Padre Pio while confessions were going on. If he were confessing the women in the open confessional in the church itself, they could actually see him. If, instead, it was the men, in the sacristy, in a species of screened cubicle, though he could not be seen he was near at hand, and they might catch a glimpse of him or even get his blessing as he made his way back to the monastery.

After his Mass, Padre Pio's day and that of the pilgrims who had come to see him revolved chiefly around his confessional.

But there were other fixed points in the day when one shared in his presence and in his life.

In later years, when he began to be afflicted by arthritis, he no longer distributed Communion in the course of the morning. This was done by the other friars. But in former days the old church would be packed as, around ten o'clock, the men received Communion from his hands on the altar steps, and the women afterward at the altar rails.

A saintly woman once told me that, knowing how Padre Pio looked into one's very soul, she was always terrified that he would pass her over because he saw her unworthiness!

As a matter of fact, though from the expression on his face not for that reason, I did once see him pass a man by. He was a peasant, and he knelt there bemused for a moment till a companion of his whis-

pered something in his ear. At this he made a gesture which implied "Of course! What a fool I am!"
and descended the steps. My surmise was that, fasting from midnight being then still obligatory, he had
been to the early Mass, had then broken his fast,
and had forgotten about it. Whether or not, he obviously realized why he had been passed over and
found it right.

After Communion the men would gather again in
the sacristy to receive once more a word, a glance,
or a blessing from him. Poor man! He was always
"on stage," never left alone. But he accepted it as
part of his mission, always with warmheartedness
and compassion, sometimes with humor. Once, as
he was removing his surplice, it ripped at the shoulder, and a youth standing behind him exclaimed:
"Oh, Father, you've torn it!" Whereupon Padre Pio
gave him his slow smile and replied, "A tattered
flag, young man, does honor to the captain!"

I was in the sacristy after Communion one day in
the company of Father Charles Carty, the American
"radio priest" and author of one of his best-known
biographies. The look of respect and affection in
Father Carty's eye was truly touching, and I realized
what a privilege he had considered it to write that
widely read book upon him, and to give those numerous lectures on him which had sometimes had
spectacular reactions, causing people to change their
lives forthwith, and in quite a number of instances
to embrace the Catholic faith. Father Carty was dynamic and articulate, but it was not so much his
powers of reasoning which convinced people as his
earnest faith and the goodness of his heart, of which
he was at that moment giving testimony.

Another fixed point in the day was Padre Pio's afternoon Benediction of the Blessed Sacrament in church, preceded by the Rosary, and sometimes by a sermon given by some guest Capuchin preacher.

The Rosary was a quiet recitation in which the congregation was led by one of the friars. Its piety was cool and recollected. Then came the singing of the Litany of Loreto, partly by Mary Pyle's village choir, with Mary at the organ, and partly by the congregation. The music, the singing, the increased illumination of the church, and the placing of the lighted candles on the altar all produced a feeling of expectancy to which one was accustomed on church festivals. Now, however, it was charged with a deeper emotion; and when Padre Pio placed the Host in the monstrance for our adoration, everyone had reached a state of perception and true proportion not generally experienced elsewhere. People *meant* their singing and their responses; and they realized Who was blessing them as Padre Pio took the monstrance and made the Sign of the Cross above their bowed heads. Then too, as at his Mass, one could almost physically feel the people joining themselves to this suffering saint, that their aspirations and supplications might thereby be made more acceptable to God. And they *were* more acceptable, not just because of Padre Pio's merits and intercession, but because of their own more clear-eyed faith.

Benediction closed Padre Pio's public day, and the majority of pilgrims retired to their various abodes, where over their evening meal they would discuss all the experiences and insights that the day had brought to them. Some fortunate few, if they had not had the luck to see Padre Pio personally in the morning, might be able to see him now, before, after, or during his evening conference with his immediate lay collaborators. And those are other stories.

The day had its variables, too, during the hours when Padre Pio was not confessing or officiating. One made quiet visits to the church and thought of many things. During one of these visits I would make a mental note of all the situations that required his good offices, all the friends who had asked me to remember them and their petitions down there, so that when the opportunity came, instead of reeling off a long list of individual "intentions," as I had heard done, I should be able to ask him simply to pray for my intentions in general and not waste his time. And a waste of time it would have been, because, having made my general request on one occasion and realized afterward that two people had been forgotten, I determined to ask his prayers for them specifically when taking leave of him. So, during a pause, I began to say, "And then, Padre . . ." but he interrupted me smilingly and said, "Yes, I shall remember your friends too!"

Sometimes in the course of my stay I would take a brisk, longish afternoon walk down to the main village and on to the cemetery and, having paused a moment at the tomb of Padre Pio's parents and of others that I knew were dear to him, I would spend what many would be surprised to hear of as an interesting time among the other tombs and family monuments. But anyone who knows Italian cemeteries, and especially those of southern Italy, will feel no surprise. The Italians, and especially those of the south, are devoted to their dead and have many picturesque ways of, as it were, bridging the gap and holding onto them.

I spent many absorbing hours in the hospital, both while it was in process of construction and when it was functioning; yet others in the offices of the *Bollettino;* many others visiting Abresch's well-stocked and serious premises, where there were books on Padre Pio, pictures and postcards of him, as well as of the church and hospital, records of his Benediction prayers, and the whole range of religious statues, rosaries, medals, medallions, etc., common to "repositories" all over the world. Here, or in other similar shops, one got one's little souvenirs for self and friends, and the religious objects that one wanted Padre Pio to bless.

The most pleasant evenings I passed in San Giovanni were those spent in the Sanguinetti home, with the doctor and his sweet, charming, intelligent wife. After the doctor's death, when Marisa Paolucci of the hospital laboratory staff had come to share that home with her, I continued on each visit to go there. To this day my wife and I are in correspondence with the Signora Emilia, and every one of her letters across the years, with all the news of Padre Pio and of San Giovanni, we have affectionately kept.

After Gino Ghisleri had entered the scene and built a house for his daughter and son-in-law and their children, many were the happy and fascinating hours spent in that house too. "Puppa" all wife and mother; "Pippo" with the breeziness and dash for his medical and mayoral work that he displayed on the top-League football field in his recent youth; Gino, the by now patriarchal figure—but a very zesty patriarch; and Carmen, his patient, sweet-natured Belgian wife—all of them wholly dedicated to Padre Pio and to his work, all of them with typical Padre Pio incidents and episodes to relate.

Sometimes there would be a late fireside chat with some fellow pilgrim in the hotel before retiring.

All in all, from the foregoing it should, I think, be obvious that at San Giovanni one breathed, spoke, lived in a world completely different from the one left behind in city or village, no matter where.

Since Padre Pio's death I have never gone back, and, despite the old friends who are down there, I never will. With them too, as with Padre Pio, I am joined in spirit; and one of these days we shall meet again.

For those who lived permanently alongside Padre Pio at San Giovanni, the matter is different. They had the inestimable privilege of having him with them daily in the flesh all those years, and they became an integral part of his little physical world. Now he has moved out of that physical world, where they remain, and they have him in their hearts and in the memories that illumine each familiar thing which was familiar to him too, and they have a tomb to honor.

But I want no part of any tomb. For those of us who saw Padre Pio physically only during our visits, he was always still with us when we were far away— but really with us. Even though he was living his life in his Gargano monastery, and even if we did not see him in bi-location or regularly receive his wonderful perfume, we knew that he was there, conscious of our needs, listening to us, eager to protect us, trying to guide us along the path to his Master—

even when often in our blindness we did not want to follow it. For us, for me, he is still very much alive. If I ever forget it, it is not for long, for a painting or a photograph of him is never far away. Nothing has changed. He is still alongside, knowing he is needed. He has more time now for all those who look to him; and bi-location must now seem to him a very slow and clumsy operation indeed!

However, I should love to see the large crowds of new pilgrims who flock today to San Giovanni from all parts of the world and keep on increasing. They cannot but draw inspiration from visiting that tomb, from seeing the enduring monuments to him in monastery and church and hospital, from viewing the places that he sanctified by his warm presence for over half a century. I know that "virtue will go out from him" there—though not alone there—to all who continue to seek him; and that they will come away with new faith and strength, and with their crosses lightened.

CHAPTER XX

I said that Padre Pio's day revolved chiefly around his confessional; and it is, I believe, as a confessor more than for anything else that he would wish to be remembered. Hour after hour, day after day, week after week he sat there, for fifty long years.

He did not eat at all, except for a spoonful of soup or a forkful of spaghetti, or rice, or vegetables in the refectory once a day under obedience; and for a man who should have been dehydrated by the life he led, what he drank too was minimal. He rose long before four o'clock to prepare for his Mass; and God knows at what hour he had stretched himself on his poor bed for what, as we shall see, it would be wrong to call sleep. All day and every day he was under the gaze, subjected to the supplications of a multitude of persons who had come to him in urgent quest of help. He had his Rule to follow; he was spiritual director to the Community; he had his helpers to listen to and advise on the hospital, the *Bollettino,* the massive correspondence, and so on. He had his world-wide family to keep in touch with, via celestial satellite, we might say; and sometimes, as we have seen, in full bi-location. On top of that he bore continuously in his body the wounds and sufferings of Christ.

Even without the long, fatiguing hours of concentration in the confessional, where his direct contacts with weak, sinful, suffering humanity principally took place, it was an existence that the greatest human strength could not have stood up to for long. With his endless penitents thrown in, each of them considering himself or herself a special individual requiring all his attention, and with the special attention that he did effectively give to all of them, it was a life which without his complete immersion in God would have been absolutely impossible to bear. But for fifty years he bore it in the intense heat and bitter cold of the Gargano mountainside.

How was he as a confessor? All things to all men, paternally. Where tenderness was needed, it flowed out from him. Where help and prompting were required, they were given. Where bracing and strengthening were called for, they were provided. All sincere men and women were at once enveloped in the mantle of his sanctity. They came away not only cleansed but, in the sensing of his remoteness from sin and why, more keenly aware of what sin really meant.

Many said he could be gruff and irate, that he would at times snap shut the panel in the penitent's face, that he could demolish a penitent with a searing phrase.

It is true. All things to all men. He recognized immediately insincerity, hypocrisy, or falsehood, and struck at it. But it was not out of pique or vindictiveness. He loved souls too deeply for that. It was his way of netting his fish. Where he had been rough or angry, the penitent would be found later to have returned in more correct or chastened dispositions and would be received accordingly.

I saw a handsome young American priest explode

in anger when Padre Pio refused to hear his confession and, when he insisted, treated him roughly in front of others. "What?" he said, after Padre Pio had gone. "He may be Padre Pio, but I too am a priest and he has no right to treat me in such fashion!"

I was able to introduce myself, and asked him if he would dine with me in the hotel that night. "Thank you—yes!" he fumed. "But only because I have no means of getting off from here before tomorrow morning!"

At dinner he was still very hurt and angry. He told me that as a student in Rome he had come on two occasions to San Giovanni, and that as a priest in the States he tried to make the reading of his office coincide with the time of Padre Pio's saying Mass. He was a fine young priest, full of good will, but I thought maybe a little lacking in sensitivity toward the local scene. I felt that perhaps Padre Pio thought so too. A priest at San Giovanni could give scandal where he would not give it in New York or Los Angeles. He should not, for instance, drink a whiskey and smoke a *cigarillo* in public, as I had found him doing in the bar where we met.

My attempt to pour oil took the form of asking him whether he had hitherto believed in Padre Pio. Of course he had. And did he not then think that maybe there was some fault in him that needed correction rather than in Padre Pio? I assured him that this was a case of experience speaking; when on occasion I had found Padre Pio cold and distant toward me, I had swiftly and rightly come to that conclusion. "The situation with me now is," I told him, "that if Padre Pio expressed a desire to walk all over me, I should flatten myself on the ground and invite him to start walking." He got the point at once; and I rejoice to say that not only did Padre Pio receive him in his cell next morning, confess him, and accept him as a spiritual son, but, as a personal bonus, a deep bond of friendship grew up between that priest and his fellow diner and, to the great spiritual benefit of the latter, it continues happily unto this day.

Carlo Campanini, the Italian humorous actor of whom I have spoken, gave a characteristically mirth-provoking account of a confessional episode. I cannot reproduce all Campanini's quick-fire comments and asides, or his imitations in dialect of the *dramatis personae,* but here are the bones of this typical piece of San Giovanni dramatic relief.

On a winter's day in the old church, when there were not too many people there, Campanini had been lending a hand in sorting out the order of precedence among the waiting men. There arrived a trio of newcomers from Naples: a caricature of the traditional "Big Boss" figure and two lieutenants. When they had taken in the situation and realized that the way to hold converse with Padre Pio was to enter the confessional, one of the lieutenants approached Campanini and suggested that, since *Il Commendatore* was a very important man and had little time, he should be permitted to jump the queue and go in at once. "Everybody is a *commendatore* here," said Campanini. "He'll just have to take his turn."

The *commendatore*, recognizing an aura of social self-confidence in the man who had passed this judgment, decided to enter into conversation with him while he waited, and had a lot of questions to ask. Quite clearly he either had his confession at his fingertips or was taking it with a certain nonchalance. At length his turn came, and he entered. He did not have time to kneel. There was a roar, as from a wounded lion, and the *commendatore* came shooting out, as Campanini put it, "like a bullet from a gun!"

Shaken and confused, he made his way back to him. "What kind of a blackguardly monk is that?" he asked. "Why?" "He did not give me time to say a word," said he, "but straightway called me an old pig and told me to get out!" "Well," said Campanini, "you must know more about why he called you that than I. He certainly had his own good reasons." "I can't think why," rejoined the other, and then, after a pause, "unless it is because I happen to be living with a woman who is not my wife!" "It just could be that," said Campanini dryly. "It would not surprise me!"

I do not know how this confessional story of a non-penitent ended up, even in the short term. We can only hope for the *commendatore,* and be quite certain that Padre Pio knew shock treatment was the therapy indicated. I do, however, know the outcome of another such story.

It befell the brother of a girl who was a student of mine at Genoa University before the last war. He was very justly considered to be the bad hat of the family, and the story of how he fetched up at San Giovanni is well known and amazing. When he got there and eventually made his way to the confessional, he could think of nothing better to do than to say he was not there to confess but to ask prayers for a relative who was gravely ill. This was untrue, and his way of testing the alleged "miracle man." He got results at once, for Padre Pio struck him across the face and ordered him out.

This instantaneous ejection landed him squarely on "the road to Damascus"; for, after wandering for some time on the mountain paths above the monastery, he came back to ask pardon and made a proper and sincere confession. When he left San Giovanni, Padre Pio's parting instruction to him was: "You have been given bread; go now and share it with others." He did, most widely. And he it was who was guided by one of Padre Pio's "perfume indicators," outside a Genoese art gallery, to find Francesco Messina, the sculptor, whose life style was thereby abruptly changed, who became one of Padre Pio's most fervent disciples, and whose bronze Stations of the Cross on the hillside are now a path of meditation for most pilgrims who go to San Giovanni Rotondo.

Perhaps I can conclude these tales of the confessional by recounting that of my old Capuchin confessor in Milan, Padre Gian Antonio.

When I told him that I had been to see Padre Pio, he was delighted. "Were you able to speak to him?" he asked. "For an hour!" "For an *hour?* Come out to the cloisters and tell me about it!" "Just a moment," I replied. "Despite all your descriptions of him, I went down there fighting against the whole idea of the journey. I asked myself, if Christ is present in every tabernacle, what need have I to go to the south of Italy to see a fellow man?" "Excellent reasoning!" he observed. "But now you have been there; now you know that he helps you to *approach* that tabernacle." "Exactly, Father. And in my apparent logic lay my presumption." "Ah, well," said he, "let me tell you of *my* first visit."

He told me then of his long journey down and of his arrival in a bullock wagon over a road that was little better than the bed of a river. Padre Pio had received the stigmata only a short time before, and the Capuchin world was in various ways stirred by the news.

The thing he at once realized, he said, was that the case was genuine; for he was staying in the monastery and saw the deep respect with which Padre Pio was treated by the other friars. People outside the monastery could have been mistaken or misled, he said, but not they.

Eventually he was confessed by him; and he told me that as he came out he felt as if he was walking on air. "Then," said he, "I took hold of myself. 'Why are you so happy?' I asked myself. 'Because you have been confessed by Padre Pio? Why, certainly, he was an admirable confessor and gave you excellent counsel. But you have been to other good confessors before and received much similar good advice. The fact of the matter is that you should be walking on air, not merely now, but *each* time that you come out from confession!"

"And that," he said, "was Padre Pio's first little lesson for me."

CHAPTER XXI

To go to San Giovanni was, as I have tried to depict, to enter another world—on *any* visit. They were *all* special. But some were more special than others; or at least they were to me.

The tale I am about to recount, for instance, may well contain little of outstanding interest for the average reader, but the memory of the visit it describes gives me a very great deal of pleasure, and I shall put it down and hope for the best.

I had managed to get away for a brief visit on the feast of Corpus Christi. This feast takes place at a lovely season of the year, and its open-air processions of the Blessed Sacrament with Benediction given at flower-decked altars along the route used to be a striking feature of the liturgical year.

At San Giovanni there was a big procession that day, with bands, and little white-clad girls strewing the road with flowers before the passage of the monstrance under its canopy. Alas, though I had managed to get into the monastery, I had not yet been able to speak with Padre Pio when the order was given for everyone, both friars and visitors, to go out and join the procession.

After the procession there would be a solemn ceremony in the church, and I knew it would be impossible to see him before having to leave and catch the Rome train. So I hid. I slipped into the "Choir" of the old church and stayed there until the silence told me that everyone, save Padre Pio, had gone. Padre Pio could not possibly be expected to walk in the long procession on those wounded feet of his and would be in his cell. Quietly I made my way back along the corridor again and waited in an alcove. Complete silence filled the place except for the ticking of the old monastery clock.

As I stood there, I was in a state of advanced trepidation, because I knew well Padre Pio's respect for rules and how he could give me, if he thought it necessary, the most soul-shaking dressing down. It was something to daunt even the stoutest heart!

However, as the moments ticked by, I began to prepare a plea for the defense and, as this progressed, I became more and more convinced of the injustice of any accusations that might be leveled against me. There was a solemn peroration wherein I was to explain that if it had been a question of assisting at the procession of "Gesù Sacramentato" I could well have stayed on in Milan; whereas I had come here to where I believed that a corner of the veil was for a moment lifted for us. It seemed good to me, and I was particularly happy with the phrase "Gesù Sacramentato," which was one I had never used before.

At last there was a step in the corridor, I emerged from the alcove, and there was Padre Pio looking at me. All the fine phrases evaporated and I merely dropped on one knee to kiss his hand and said, "Now, Padre, please don't give me any 'head-washing [*lavata di testa*]!'" "No, no," said he very kindly. "Let us go into the parlor here and talk." I could not believe my ears.

"And how are you keeping now, Padre?" "Let us thank God," said he. (It was his habitual response to any query after his health; for how could he possibly say that he was well without offending the truth?) I had a long, happy, interesting conversation with him to brighten up life and its empty presumptions for a while; and then, as the sound of music was heard in the distance, he arose to embrace me and give his farewell salutation of "May the Angel of the Lord accompany you always!" Then he added, with a twinkle, "Gesù Sacramentato is now approaching. You will be able to have Benediction in front of the hospital before you leave!"

I went down the monastery staircase not just walking on air like Padre Gian Antonio, but with the largest of grins. For it was quite clear to me that the prisoner's speech from the dock had been duly noted.

CHAPTER XXII

On the particular occasion I speak of now I arrived in San Giovanni feeling ill and absolutely bone tired; so after the early Mass, instead of seeking him out in the sacristy, I went back to bed and did not see him until he rose from the confessional at midday. "What!" he called in mock dudgeon. "Is this the time to report to your commanding officer?" Then came the fatherly embrace, and as I write I can still feel that grizzled beard, the rough cloth of his habit, and the smell of snuff!

It was Saturday. "How long are you staying?" he asked. "Till Monday morning, Padre." "Always the same," was his reply. "You are hardly here till you are off again. Tell me, what is your Christian name?" "Giovanni, Padre." "That is right; and next Friday is your feast day [June 24, feast of St. John the Baptist]. Will you remain and spend it here?"

Now at that time I was engaged in some amateurish farming on the west coast of Ireland, where my wife and I now live permanently, and I used to come to Italy thrice a year, for a six- or seven-week stay, to look after some business interests I had left behind me there. I was due to return to Ireland in a fortnight's time, and a number of meetings had already been arranged in Milan and elsewhere, while others were due to be set up. Consequently, taken by surprise and aware of the commitments, I instinctively hedged.

"But, Padre, I have to go back to Ireland." "Yes," he rejoined, "but not next week. Otherwise I should not have asked you."

His obvious knowledge of my schedules, without any divulgence of them by me, jerked me back into reality. "Padre," I assured him, "if you were to ask me to return to Ireland now walking on my hands, I should get my feet up in the air immediately and start off! If you want me to, just imagine if I won't stay here for another week." "H'm," said he, "we'll see."

That was certainly a week to remember. I saw and heard things I had never seen or heard there before, and some of them will be duly recounted. It was also a week of great advancement in Padre Pio's friendship and confidence; and afterward, as an outcome of this, he entrusted me with missions which gave me the opportunity to make some small return for all his immense benefactions. Some of that too will come later.

On the eve of St. John's a group of us were talking to him in the corridor outside his cell at the end of the day. He turned to me and said, "Beh, Giovanni, tomorrow is your feast day, and at Mass I shall be remembering you and your wife and family." And then, looking around, "But, you know, you are not the only Giovanni here. Here," pointing them out, "we have Giovanni Telfner" (the count already referred to) "and Giovanni Vignolini" (his infirmarian).

Now both Giovannis were thin as rakes, so with an ample gesture around my middle, I replied, "Ah, yes, Padre. But these are very slim Giovannis. The only real Giovanni *Rotondo* here is me!"

Padre Pio joined in the general mirth; but underneath his banter I felt that all was not well with him. He was right at the end of his resources. He had told me I could come in for a chat, and I went in before him. He gave the others his blessing, closed the door, and then, as he came away from it. I suddenly saw him begin to crumple. I caught him before he fell to the floor and assisted him to a chair.

As he sat there waiting to recover, pale as a sheet and obviously completely drained of strength, I happened to notice his ankles. They were incredibly swollen, and again I remembered, as we all invariably forgot, on what feet he had to stand and move around all day.

Then the thought of the season of intense heat now approaching came to me. He bore in his body, as we shall learn, not only the visible open wounds of the nails and spear, but the sufferings from the scourging and crowning with thorns; and the pain of the weight of his habit upon the invisible weals under the heat of the summer sun could at least be guessed at, as likewise the distress caused by things like the weight of his heavy Benediction vestment in a packed summer church. I had seen him wince a little even from the sun playing on his back through a window in the monastery corridor.

"Poor Padre!" I exclaimed spontaneously. "The hot days are almost here." And it was then that I received his first real confidence; for generally no word of his wounds or sufferings ever passed his lips. "No," said he in a weary voice. "It is not so much the days. You see, when the events of the day

begin, one thing carries me on to the next, and so
the day passes. It is the nights. If ever I allow myself
to sleep, the pain of these" (and he held up his
wounded hands to indicate the stigmata) "is multi-
plied beyond measure."

"Poor Padre" indeed. This too he had to bear in
the accompanying of his Lord and the succoring of
his brethren.

But next day, as happened so regularly, he
seemed renewed; and in the afternoon when he received Gino Ghisleri and myself in his cell, with
shameless brashness I took advantage of his smiling
welcome. "Padre, isn't it customary for fathers to
give their sons a present on their feast day?" He
gave me a keen glance. "Let's hear!" said he. "Well,
I thought, maybe, you know, a little 'holy picture'
with a message, just a small message, to bring back
to my wife." "Ah, now," said he, "that is a present I
shall give you with the greatest pleasure." He did;
and another for myself, and one each for Gino and
his wife, when Gino asked to become a Giovanni for
the day and be included.

As he wrote them I had a considerable twinge of
conscience, for the effort required of him to hold the
pen was unconsciously underlined in the jutting
movement he made with his chin as he formed the
words. He then laughed at the resultant "scrawls,"
as he called them, and asked whether he should
translate them for us. But we managed to read them
without his assistance and thanked him profusely;
and it has ever since been a double pleasure for me
each time I open my old Latin missal and see that
"scrawl," with underneath it "P. Pio, Capp."

CHAPTER XXIII

A sad and exceptional visit to San Giovanni was made a month or so after the death of Dr. Sanguinetti.

I arrived late on a Sunday afternoon and met Padre Pio after Benediction. He was coming slowly and painfully along the corridor, being helped by two of his fellow friars; and there were small knots of priests and laymen waiting to speak to him. He looked completely broken.

At our last meeting he had said, looking at the doctor and myself, "Who knows when and where we shall meet again?" and now the significance of the phrase was all too clear.

He looked up, and when he saw me, that surely was the most humbling moment of my life; for no one more than I knew just how unworthy of it I was. He came forward and embraced me, weeping, put my arm through his and, turning to the others, said: "This is my friend."

Although I was very confused, I must confess also to experiencing a great glow of happiness. Afterward I accepted it in the thought that, firstly, he said it because of my close association with his *real* friend, the doctor, and, secondly, that, valueless and unimportant though my friendship for him might be and was, at least it was total and sincere.

I went into the little parlor with him and when we

had sat down said, "And so, Padre, we have lost our old friend." He nodded without speaking, and the tears coursed down his cheeks. "But, Padre, you know he has gone to his great reward." "Ah, yes," said he, "he has indeed. But you know, not only the mind but the human heart claims its share." I thought of how Christ had wept over Lazarus; and how the bystanders had said, "Look at Him; see how He loved him."

He looked at me, still stricken by that tremendous absence, and said, "Well, never did you think you would see Padre Pio reduced to this." "Now," I told him, "if possible, I respect Padre Pio more than I did before, because I see him in his human frailty." He shook his head and was not to be comforted.

Several times I sat and talked with him during that visit, and each time attempted to lift him out of this extra suffering. It seemed all to no avail.

On the last occasion I mentioned conversationally that there was a new and very interesting little book out in Ireland and that many people were reading it. He asked me with reluctance, guessing what the answer would be, "A book about what?" "I'll give you two guesses, Padre," I replied cheerfully, hoping to spark off his jocularity. Not a flicker. On the contrary, his eyes filled again with tears, and he said, "You are all so mistaken. All of you. It is you who are good, not I." "Well," I answered, "please leave us with our illusions, because we are very fond of them." His reply was serious and emphatic. "Listen. God made all things. His creation includes the stars and the humblest domestic utensil. I belong to the second category."

When I attempted to remonstrate, he interrupted

me and went on: "Don't think I am using rhetoric or speaking out of false modesty. I realize to the full the greatness of the gifts that God has bestowed upon me. But that terrifies me, because I know only too well what miserable use I have made of them. If He had given them to the lowest scoundrel in the world, he would have employed them better. I dread the thought of death and having to answer for it." His eyes looked into mine, dark with the intensity of trying to convey the sincerity of what he was saying.

Still no good; in fact worse. I told him I understood all this in the light of something I had heard the great moral theologian, Vermeersch, say in a lecture hall of the Gregorian University. "You might think," Vermeersch had told his students, "that the terrible death scene is that of a man who dies in terror. It is not. I have seen men who had lived lives of sanctity and penance behind monastery walls die like that—terrified. I had been their confessor and knew they had souls as clear as crystal. I realized that this was their last trial, the end of their Purgatory, and that their souls would go straight to heaven. No; the dreadful death to witness is that of the man concerning whom you have the moral certainty that he is in a state of mortal sin, and who is going with tranquility before his Maker because, having strangled the voice of conscience long years ago, it is no longer there to speak to him. That is a truly terrible death!"

When Padre Pio heard the name of Vermeersch, he was at once interested and listened very attentively to what I related. At the end he nodded solemnly and thoughtfully and then said: "Terrible indeed! And yet, and yet, I believe that not a great

number of souls go to hell. God loves us so much.
He formed us in His image. God the Son incarnate
died to redeem us. He loves us beyond understanding. And it is my belief that even when we
have passed from the consciousness of this world,
when we appear to be dead, God, before He judges
us, will give us a chance to see and understand what
sin really is. And if we understand it properly, how
could we fail to repent?"

"Let us hope, Padre, that that is the way it will
be," I said to him; and then, still trying hard to con-
jure up a smile from him, "but don't let's pass the
word around."

There was no smile; so I made one last effort on
another tack and tried to shock him out of his
sadness.

"Do you remember the Irish Jesuit writer, Father
Nash, who came to see you?" His face lit up at the
memory. "Yes, indeed I do. How is he?" "He is
well, Padre. His Superior was up in Donegal recently, and I met him just before I came away. Do
you know what he asked me?" The light died in his
eyes, and he looked at me with distrustful melan-
choly, anticipating another attack on his humility.
"What did he ask?" "Well, I was telling him about
San Giovanni and all the thousands of people who
came here from all over the world"—(a restive, un-
comfortable movement from him)—"and what he
said was: 'Poor man, how does his humility stand up
to it?'"

That was a very insolent thing to say to Padre
Pio, but I knew it would result in *some* kind of
strong reaction; and so, like a surgeon making a

deep incision, I said it. The result was beyond anything I had hoped for.

He looked at me with absolute incredulity for some seconds, and then he began to laugh, but to laugh more heartily than I had ever seen him do before. He shook with mirth. "My humility? . . . My *humility?*" He repeated the phrase as he laughed. He thought it the funniest joke he had ever heard in his whole life.

At length, when his laughter had subsided, he said with a return of his old spirit: "When you next see that Jesuit Superior, will you please tell him from me that I hope I am neither mad nor a thief. And if I were to attribute to myself what belongs obviously and exclusively to God alone, there could be no other answer. I should have to be one or the other, either mad or a thief!"

He paused, and then went on: "Don't you see? It is as if someone here gave you a beautiful gold watch to take up to Milan to be repaired, and during the journey you took it out and displayed it as your own to the other occupants of the compartment. Wouldn't you be a very foolish fellow? Or, if you actually then meant to keep it, wouldn't you be a very wicked one?" He added, "You tell the Superior that!" and then jocularly, with a shake of his head, "Ah, those Superiors!"

I felt that that human heart of his, to which he had made reference, had at last begun to get over its grief; and that nobody would be more pleased about this than the good doctor, who, with his own big heart, had in the past helped him carry his burdens so often.

CHAPTER XXIV

Another trip to San Giovanni stands out, not because of any experience of mine, but because of what happened to another person.

There was a man whom I had seen there with his wife on three or four consecutive visits, and I found that they had taken up temporary residence in the village. He suffered from a throat cancer which was becoming steadily worse, and at length he was able to speak only in a hoarse, barely intelligible whisper.

He had come down from Milan seeking a cure, but his faith and constancy were to be sorely tried. A whole year passed. He went regularly to confession to Padre Pio. Sometimes he was able to speak with him in the monastery. But, as well as that, day in and day out he would be present in the sacristy and would unfailingly await his passing from monastery to church and back; and on these occasions he would just look at him, willing him, silently imploring him, to obtain his cure. He meant not to give in until his last gasp.

Now that is the kind of faith which does eventually move mountains; and after overcoming blankness, and suffering, and despair, he got his reward.

He told me that once, when he had gone to bed early, the pain, the sensation of smothering, and the temptation to despair were so great that he leaped from bed, dressed hastily, and practically ran to the monastery door. The outside door was closed for the night, but he rang the bell until one of the friars appeared. He was told that it was impossible to see Padre Pio at this hour and that he was in choir with the rest of the Community; but such was his distress and desperation that the friar took pity upon him and brought him up.

Naturally, the spectacle of this half-crazed man, whom they all knew and pitied, stopped the recitation of the office, and in the ensuing silence Padre Pio left his place and came toward him. It must indeed have been a dramatic scene.

Weeping and distraught, he threw himself upon his knees. Padre Pio laid his hand on his head. He then told me that not only did the pain and the distress at once disappear, but his whole being was filled with such a sensation of pleasure that after a moment he felt he could bear it no longer and that he would die. He tore Padre Pio's hand from his head and got from him in return an uncomplaining, understanding smile and the words: "Wasn't that beautiful? Now go back to bed and sleep."

(The inference of this episode would seem to be that the sick man received a foretaste of some of the lesser joys of Paradise, which it would be logical to think that the body in its present imperfect state would be incapable of experiencing without dissolution.)

Some time later I was down on a visit when our friend came to me radiant, quite certain now that he was about to be cured, for in his low, hoarse whisper he informed me that Padre Pio had told him to go to Bologna and be operated on there by a well-known surgeon. I accompanied him on the train as far as Bologna, and though he was happy and confident, his physical distress was still with him, and regularly he had to go and open a window in the corridor to receive (I presume) further impetus for his breathing.

The next time I saw him was in my office in Milan, in the company of Campanini, the comedian, and a man from Lecco whose case had been even more sensational. As he sat there on the other side of my desk, he was smoking Lucky Strike cigarettes and speaking in the robust tones which were his naturally. So far as he was concerned, the surgeon had merely been an instrument used by Padre Pio, for whatever recondite reason, and I for one would certainly not disagree with him.

CHAPTER XXV

Let me tell of the man from Lecco. He was sitting in my office looking at me with two perfectly ordinary-looking eyes. The only extraordinary thing about them was that until some months previously they had been like dried, shriveled peas in his head, and he had been totally blind.

I had never met him before but had learned every detail of his case from Gino Ghisleri, who had been present when on his knees he had begged Padre Pio to restore his sight "even if only in one eye," that he might again see the faces of his dear ones. After repeating questioningly "Only in one eye?" Padre Pio had told him to be of good heart and that he would pray for him.

Gino said that this had been one of the most moving spectacles he had witnessed in San Giovanni, but that it had been completely outshone some weeks later when the blind man returned with his sight restored and his two eyes of completely normal appearance. He had been there again when the man from Lecco once more knelt, this time with tears of happiness, to thank his benefactor.

"So," said Padre Pio, "you are now seeing normally again?" "Yes," replied the man, "from this eye here, not from the other." "Ah!" came the response. "Only from *one* eye? Let that be a lesson to you. Never put limitations on God. Always ask for the big grace!"

This tale I now heard first hand from the person concerned. He and his friend now told me their detailed experiences, how their cures had occurred and progressed, and I listened, fascinated.

At the end, however, Campanini surprised us all by turning to them and saying, "All terrific! All fantastic! But remember that neither of you had a cure like mine!" "What?" one of them replied. "What cure did you have?" "You, my friend, were cured of cancer of the throat," he said. "Absolute child's play! I was healed of cancer of the soul. That, believe me, is a miracle much more difficult to achieve."

There was a silence, and he told us then of his own life, of his conversion by Padre Pio, of his relapse for several years, and of his return.

CHAPTER XXVI

It is fitting that the last of the "special" visits to San Giovanni to be recounted should be that which lengthened the course of my own life. It has, at any rate, to be told.

It was in the early days of my acquaintance with Padre Pio. I had arranged to meet Douglas Woodruff and several other friends in Rome; there were five or six of us. By chance, Dr. Sanguinetti was in Rome too, and we all traveled down together.

Background to the events about to be described is that toward the end of the war, owing to years of gross overstrain, I had developed heart trouble. Nothing organic so far, the doctors said, but it would have to come. I was choking at times with palpitations and often could sleep only in a sitting position. Something finally had to give, and it took the form, not of a heart attack, but of a partial stroke. I went out like a light one evening and was rushed off to hospital.

I cut the treatment short and went back to my job; and possibly because of this, when the war was over, the acute localized head pains which had presaged the stroke began to return. Twice these occurred during the night while I was in Rome, and I felt that I was coming very close to passing on. With a wife and young family, the thought was not a

pleasant one, and I decided to ask Padre Pio to intervene.

During his Mass on the first morning of the visit I
bombarded him continuously in thought, asking him
to obtain this favor for me. When he rose from the
confessional toward midday I saw him with Dr. Sanguinetti and the others in the monastery. He wasted
no time. Addressing me immediately as though I had
actually spoken to him, he said in a calm and gentle
voice, "Listen to me. My prayer for you is that you
go to heaven. Let that be enough for you. And naturally, do you pray for me with the same intention.
But that is my prayer for you. Do you understand?"
"Yes, Padre."

I thought, Well, that's that. We may prepare to
pull the blinds down any day now.

He turned to speak to the others, and the conversation became general. Several times he gave me a
keen glance, and as I tried to comfort myself with
the thought that God could look after my family
much better than I could, I was quite certain I was
showing no evidence of disappointment. Maybe I
was mistaken; but anyhow, whatever the reason,
when we knelt for his blessing before he moved
along the corridor, he took a good long look at me,
said nothing, but then, taking my head between his
hands, he held it hard for quite some time against
where the wound was in his side; he then gave me
his blessing and passed along.

When he went, everyone looked at me, and
Douglas Woodruff said smilingly, "Well, it is easy to
see who is favorite around here!" I joked about this
and said that, on the contrary, it was quite clear who
was most in need of his help.

Three times I knelt for his blessing during that visit. No further word was spoken; but each time he did the same thing, holding my head hard against his side. Two months or so later I was down again and kneeling for his blessing once more. He took my head, placed it for an instant against his side, and then, pushing it away with a pleased, playful expression like that of a good-humored family doctor who finds his patient fully restored to health, he waited for me to stand up and embraced me. That was almost twenty-five years ago: almost twenty-five years of borrowed time during which I have never had the slightest recurrence of my trouble.

But the story does not end there. I said that during the war I had had heart problems. They were still around, but I had never asked Padre Pio's intervention in the matter. However, two or three times, after the above happenings, in the course of normal conversation, without any relevant reference, he placed the palm of his right hand, and therefore its wound, against my heart. Since then, not only have I put this unfortunate organ under very severe stresses without any ill result, but on the several occasions on which I have had general medical examinations, the doctor in each case has said after his sounding, "Nothing wrong with your *heart*, anyway!"

Finally, those who have lived strenuous lives and are advanced in years will know well with what displeasure one sees this or that shadow of malfunction threatening one's activities. Spoiled, perhaps, by Padre Pio's indulgence, each time I felt the situation warranted it, I had the shameless presumption to call out again to him for help—each time only in thought, without a word being spoken. Each time, unfailingly, the help came. And when my last mental request to him had been formulated, he looked at me again with that by now amused smile which told me he had got the message, and said: "Giovanni, Giovanni, by dint of planting new vines, you will make yourself a whole new vineyard!"

Well, one of these days, and it cannot be too far distant, the vines will have withered and the vineyard be no more. But meantime, to my family and me it has given wonderful harvests of grapes for which each one of us will be forever grateful. So let me close this chapter now by saying again, most sincerely: Thank you once more for everything, Padre Pio.

CHAPTER XXVII

So far these tales concerning Padre Pio have been chiefly of his concrete interventions on behalf of others or of episodes and situations directly regarding him. There were, however, chapters on Dr. Sanguinetti and Gino Ghisleri, who collaborated so magnificently in his work; and now I should like to tell of some of the other people I met at San Giovanni. Some were visitors like myself; others, like the Sanguinettis and the Salas, had forsaken their homes, their friends, and all the familiar things, to participate in Padre Pio's life and apostolate here in the isolated, stony uplands of the Gargano Peninsula. That required generosity and self-sacrifice in abundant, sometimes heroic, measure.

One truly heroic soul whom I met for the first and only time on the eve of her death was Signorina Elena Bandini. Through Gino Ghisleri and the doctor who was then medical superintendent of the hospital, Dr. Gusso, I knew a great deal about her. She had lived here for many years, doing what she could for church, monastery, and the local populace, and now she had been dying for a long time of painful stomach cancer. After all his recent sojourns to complete and launch the hospital, Gino had spoken of her with a mixture of affection, admiration, and awe. Her sufferings were intense but she asked for

no cure. She wanted to unite them to those of Padre
Pio and to offer them for his intentions.

Since she had become completely immobilized, it
was known and accepted quite naturally that Padre
Pio visited her from time to time, to comfort and
strengthen her, in bi-location. (One does not pass
one's daily life amid a variety of startling miracles
and find this at all out of the way.) Eventually her
sufferings were so prolonged and unbearable that
she began to ask Padre Pio to obtain her release
through the final sacrifice of her life. His reply was,
it was reported: "Just a little longer"; and on one
occasion: "Just a little more straw to burn."

Each week it seemed that she could not possibly
survive any longer; but she did. And then, one time
when Gino Ghisleri and I had gone down together
and were met at the station by Dr. Gusso, he told us
that it was now absolutely impossible she could survive. There was an incredible cavity in her body, he
said, eaten away by the disease, and since morning
she had had no fewer than fifteen hemorrhages.

"Poor, poor Elena!" said Gino; and then, to me,
"Will you come and visit her with me?" "Absolutely
not," I replied. "Poor woman, she has enough to
bear without having to make efforts at politeness to
an utter stranger." Gino was not convinced, however, and next day as we were coming down from
the hospital to our hotel for lunch he said he was
going in for a moment to see her and asked me to
wait for him in the parlor of her house. I did, and
was much oppressed by doing so, because I could
hear the piteous, subdued laments that came from
her bedroom. Suddenly, to my literal horror, Gino
came hurrying into the parlor saying, "Come on

quickly! She wants to see you!" The two doors were standing open behind him, and I could do nothing but go—as I say, horrified.

But he was right. It was an experience not to be missed and never to be forgotten. She was lying with her eyes closed. At the head of the bed sat an old woman holding a tube from an oxygen cylinder before her mouth, and every breath that she drew was also a lament—not desperate; controlled; but obviously the effect of the most intense pain. Her dark gray hair, however, was smoothly, perfectly in place; her face was almost transparent, but calm and resigned; and then she opened her eyes and gave a fleeting attempt at a smile. Those eyes were a revelation. They were blue; they were astonishingly youthful; and they possessed the crystalline purity of a child.

Then she began to speak. Each phrase was a gasp, and after each gasp there was a collapse. I tried to stop her, but to no avail. "I have heard of you. . . . You come from Ireland. . . . Ireland is a good Catholic country. . . . I am glad to have met you . . . and up there" (raising her glance slightly) "I shall shortly remember you both."

I uttered some awkward phrases, telling her what an example she had given us, and we withdrew quietly from the room as, owing to the effort of speaking, she was lying there in a more prolonged collapse than before.

Next day I went there to pray by her bedside as she lay dead, with her rosary beads entwined through fingers as translucent as her face. I prayed and looked long at that face, for I knew I had been privileged to meet another great saint just before her soul went straight to heaven.

St. Thérèse of Lisieux explained the difference between greater and lesser saints in heaven by saying that, just as a larger glass held more water than a smaller one but could not be said to be fuller, so the saints would enjoy that measure of happiness which their potential was capable of accepting. It seemed to me a very rational explanation; and after having heard of Signorina Elena Bandini's previous terrible sufferings, and having witnessed the heroic sanctity of her death, I felt sure that Padre Pio had encouraged her to continue enduring, not for any diminution of the pains of Purgatory, but that her eternal reward might be as great as possible.

In the afternoon, when I saw Padre Pio and told him I had been to pray at her bedside, two great tears rolled down his cheeks. "Padre," I said, "she certainly went without any stop from here to Paradise." "Oh," said he quietly, "with no stop at all."

Could one desire a better epitaph?

CHAPTER XXVIII

There were other women in permanent residence at San Giovanni Rotondo whose temperaments and dispositions were very different from those of Signorina Elena Bandini. In a humorous echo of the gospel phrase, the *aficionados* of San Giovanni referred to them as *"Le Pie Donne"* or, "The Holy Women." They were fanatics; not so much holy women as holy terrors. They were not quite as bad as the *Zie di San Gennaro* (the "Aunts" of St. Gennaro, patron of Naples) because, unlike San Gennaro, Padre Pio was very much with us and was able to do something about keeping them in line. But I often thought that at times they must have been a heavy cross for him.

They were emotional, superstitious, and prime examples of that category of person who hurt and angered Padre Pio by stopping at him, as it were, instead of using him as a steppingstone to God.

One could not but be amused at some of the demonstrations of their fanaticism. For instance, while they never missed a Padre Pio Mass at any season of the year, they did not relish beginning to queue for the best places at two or three o'clock in the morning during the heavy influx of summer pilgrims; they would arrive five or ten minutes before the church doors were due to open and instead of going to the end of the queue they would take up a flank position near the head of the "enemy column." As the doors opened, they would charge, break the enemy ranks, and win their way to the front row. In the old church, where Padre Pio said his Mass at the side altar of St. Francis, they were known to have surreptitiously chained a chair or stool to the altar rails the night before in order to stake a concrete claim and have a reserved seat there next morning!

Poor Mrs. Ghisleri who, during her first visit, had humbly taken her place at the church door around 2:30 A.M., suddenly found herself bowled over and trampled. One summer there was almost a diplomatic incident when the wife of a South American ambassador informed the world that during the charge of the "Holy Women" she had actually been bitten!

However, as the Church is there chiefly for sinners who require help and discipline, and less for the godly "who need no penance," so Padre Pio was there also for the "Holy Women"; and he gained further grace for himself and for them by his patience, his counsel, and his reproofs.

I don't think people realize just what priests have to put up with in the confessional; not just the unhappy chronicle of sin and halitosis, but the eccentricities, egoism, and loquacity to which they are subjected. Think of the women whose tongues are sternly held in check by their husbands, and who then find compensation in the flood of trivial narrative with which they submerge their unhappy confessors.

There was one good lady whose loquacity resembled nothing so much as the chattering of a machine gun in rapid fire. She would attempt to ambush and besiege Padre Pio with her problems; and eventually, to the immense relief of her husband, she decided to spend half of each month at San Giovanni.

The husband, poor man, meek as the dove, but rendered also as cunning as the serpent, told Padre Pio how happy he was at his wife's decision, "and might it not benefit her if she took up residence there permanently?"

As he afterward recounted with resigned laughter, Padre Pio drew back and exclaimed, "What? Ah no, my friend! I'll take fifty per cent—yes; but fair is fair, and the other fifty will be dutifully shouldered by *you!*"

CHAPTER XXIX

These were some of Padre Pio's lesser burdens, and while we can laugh at them and he could joke about them, they were often bound to be in the nature of last straws, calculated to bring him very near to breaking point. So, at least, one imagines.

But the Signorina Elena Bandini had companions at San Giovanni. As well as others already mentioned, there were women whose lives of dedication and sacrifice were worthy reflections of his own. Such a one, for instance, was the Signorina Cleonice Morcaldi.

The Signorina Morcaldi's surname has become known to me only now. Throughout the years I knew her only as she was known by all and sundry in that little world—as Cleonice.

She was one of Padre Pio's oldest disciples, a quiet dynamo of good works and a pillar of common sense. He once referred to her, when speaking to Gino Ghisleri, as "my celestial daughter." And Gino it was who first introduced me to her.

Her house was as neat and orderly as she was, with the same kind of reserve permeating it. But Gino had brought me there not just to meet her by visiting her home but to see something else; and after the initial polite conversation, with his customary blunt directness, he said, "And now, Cleonice, show him the picture!"

She hesitated for a moment but then led me to a picture which was hanging on the wall under a species of veil. She raised the veil, and there was revealed a most striking picture of Padre Pio's head and shoulders. The face was bloodstained and suffering, and on his head was a crown of thorns. However, there was something different. The thorns were not plaited into a circular shape, as always depicted upon the head of Our Lord. The crown was just a rough mass of thorns pressed down upon the top of the head. And that, if we think of it, is exactly how it must have been.

The picture had a story. It began with a pious young girl engaged to be married to a youth who had lost his faith. She told him she could not possibly go through with the marriage unless he returned to the Church. They had discussed and argued to no avail, and eventually at her suggestion, though completely cynical, he had consented to come down with her to San Giovanni Rotondo.

On their first morning they went to that very early Mass together, and during the course of it the girl was amazed to see her fiancé gazing at the altar, pale and clearly shocked. "Does this happen every day?" he whispered to her. "Yes," she replied in wonderment, ignorant of the import of his question. Only when they came out from church was his reaction explained to her. He had seen a mass of thorns on Padre Pio's head and the blood running down his face; and naturally he took it for granted that everyone else saw this too.

She was not only amazed but troubled. She thought either that he was dissembling, for some reason she did not understand, or that he had been the victim of some kind of illusion emotionally inspired. However, when, after making her confession, she spoke to Padre Pio and asked him whether her fiancé had really seen what he recounted, Padre Pio confirmed to her that he had indeed. (And this, in turn, was evidence enough for any of us that, as well as the overt stigmata of the five wounds, his body bore the hidden stigmata and sufferings of the scourging and crowning with thorns.)

The young man was duly cured of his unbelief; the story of his conversion was told to a Polish woman painter who stayed at San Giovanni for some time; and the impressive picture, with its insight into what the "crown of thorns" had clearly been, was the result. The veil was kept over the picture lest anyone unaware of its background should think it was a presumptuous substitution of the head of Padre Pio for that of Christ without any occasion or due warrant.

Cleonice produced the parish concerts and plays; and one of these latter I recall always with a smile, not for anything connected with the play itself, which was a life of St. Peter, but for a simple passing gesture on the part of a member of the audience. St. Peter had denied his Lord, and Padre Pio, who was following the drama with close attention, shook his head at this and simultaneously made the southern Italian gesture of pretending to bite the knuckle of his index finger as a demonstration of chagrin and shocked disapproval. Those who know southern Italy will recognize that gesture and be, I think, amused as I was at this spontaneous use by him of local, popular color.

CHAPTER XXX

Two more women whom I met in San Giovanni have absolute claim to a mention.

Marisa Paolucci was the person sent by Providence to share the Signora Sanguinetti's life and home after the death of her husband. It was a very fine choice; and she became devoted friend, companion, and daughter. Seldom have I known anyone of more happy, generous, and balanced disposition than she; and she will certainly receive a most affectionate, fatherly accolade from Dr. Sanguinetti when they meet, for not only has she devoted herself wholeheartedly to the service of the hospital which he built, but by her sunny nature she has comforted and cheered the long widowhood of his wife and the double exile she had to endure after the death of Padre Pio.

Few people outside San Giovanni have heard of Marisa Paolucci. But the second woman I have in mind needs no introduction, for her name is now known by multitudes of people throughout the English-speaking world. I refer to Miss Mary Pyle.

Mary Pyle was born of well-to-do parents in the United States. She was also born a practical idealist, and first gave manifest proof of this by her association with Madame Montessori, foundress of the educational system which bears her name. She became a Catholic, heard of Padre Pio, came to San Giovanni

to see for herself, and finding there her true
fulfillment, remained for the rest of her life.

Never could that young, gently nurtured American girl have imagined that she would spend the
greater part of her days in a remote Italian mountain
hamlet; but that is what happened. There she lies
buried today; and together with those of Padre Pio's
early disciples, there assuredly will her name be forever remembered.

She built quite a large house below the monastery, and it was to give hospitality to innumerable
English-speaking visitors. There too she carried out
her tasks of training the village girls in womanly arts
and crafts and in womanly dignity. She also helped
in their formal education. And it was she who
formed and played the organ for the girls' choir
which became one of the pleasantest memories that
one carried away from Padre Pio's visible realm.

Latterly, a visit to Mary Pyle by any English-
speaking pilgrims who previously knew something of
that realm became part of their normal program,
and I never met anyone who was not impressed by
the blend of sweetness and strength that went to
make her personality.

During the days of the hospital's inauguration I
took down to see her the two American heart specialists who were there, Dr. White and Dr. Wangen-
steen, and also Dr. Evans of London. She charmed
them by her relaxed and natural American approach
in this world that was so strange to them; and then,
never a respecter of persons or situations, when the
monastery bell rang out for the Angelus, Mary stood
up and recited it in English with me, while the
others stood bowed and respectful, interested but in

no way embarrassed, precisely because her action was so unaffected.

I do not know whether he ever did so, but as we strolled up to the village again afterward, Dr. Evans said to me that this had been the most amazing weekend in his entire life and that he hoped to come back one day with more leisure and in no official capacity. If he ever did, I think it would have been Mary that he would have gone to as his guide and mentor.

In one way it seems strange to me that she should no longer be there to offer hospitality to visitors. In another it seems logical that she should have preceded Padre Pio and been there, with those other old disciples, to welcome him. But in any case, as I have said, at San Giovanni—with theirs—her name will never die.

CHAPTER XXXI

Let me now speak of some of the dedicated men I met at San Giovanni Rotondo, beyond those already described, who formed part of Padre Pio's entourage.

There were, of course, the doctors; there were the quiet men who ran the administration of the hospital and that of the *Bollettino;* there were men who did odd jobs for monastery and hospital, and who were always available. There were in all a host of men whom I came to know by sight and to greet, whose names I never knew or have forgotten. But they were real and saintly men, though they would undoubtedly laugh at the latter adjective.

Some, however, I got to know well; and some became my friends.

There was the local doctor, Dr. Lotti, a man of perpetually young appearance with a large family. He had been there before any of the other doctors, and it took his calm and pleasant disposition to keep him from ever showing jealousy or resentment toward colleagues who appeared to take at least temporary precedence over him. He was the "medical continuity" around the monastery; always there; always quiet and contained; but with a smile never far from his face.

On a warm summer's Sunday evening after Benediction Padre Pio had decided to spend his short period of relaxation and discussion with collaborators and friends, not in the parlor or on the small terrace, but in the monastery garden. There was a bowling alley of the primitive kind favored in Italy for its "sporting" surface, and as the swallows swooped below the cypresses, while the rest of us sat and chatted around Padre Pio, Dr. Lotti was playing a "needle" game against a regular Neapolitan weekend visitor, who was as exuberant and extrovert as Dr. Lotti was reserved.

As the game reached its climax, conversation ceased and everyone was watching. The doctor's last throw had laid the ball right up against the jack; and his opponent's only chance was to hit that ball in such a way that his own would displace it, but itself stay immobile beside an undisturbed jack. There was complete silence, and all eyes were on the Neapolitan as, with mock gravity, he coiled up his arm. Crack! Dr. Lotti's ball shot off, the other stayed solidly on the spot, the jack did not budge, and the game was won. The Neapolitan, with the wide grin they produce in his native city, looked over, bowed, and called, *"G-r-r-razie, Padre Pio!"*

Padre Pio exploded, the others of us laughed loudly at the Neapolitan's impudence, and it seemed to me that this lighthearted implication of a miraculous intervention by one who deeply and sincerely believed in Padre Pio was wholly symbolic.

We must thank Dr. Lotti both for the small tale and for its corollary.

CHAPTER XXXII

Giovanni Vignolini I mentioned as one of the thin Giovannis present on the eve of the feast of St. John the Baptist. He certainly was thin; and he was small, gray-haired, with sharply cut features, and a stiff leg. Despite that leg, he moved around the place with a speed and agility that made one labor to keep up with him. He was like a ball of mercury, ready to shoot off in any direction when given the occasion. He was generous-natured, with a smile that flashed like his movements and with a pronounced Tuscan accent.

The hospital, with its tidal wave of doctors and departments, was too big for him, and eventually he went back to Florence. But he was one of the pioneers, one of the old originals, and as long as I live I shall remember him shooting across the *piazza* or gazing affectionately at Padre Pio as he quipped and commented—always with an evident underlying respect—in that delectable, so easily imitable Tuscan accent.

Giovanni was Padre Pio's infirmarian in those days, and this—to be allowed to minister to his wounds, to assist him in his illnesses—was a great mark of confidence and esteem. He was one of my earliest "guardian angels," one of those beneath whose friendly wing I was borne past the Father Porter and either taken along with him into Padre

Pio's cell or placed strategically in the corridor outside to await his exit.

Padre Pio had been very ill, and his infirmarian had been given a key to the monastery so that he could call there, if he thought it necessary, during the night. On the night he told me of, he went along between one and two o'clock in the morning and, going to the cell door, he listened. There was no sound from within, and thinking it would be a pity to disturb his patient if he were asleep, he decided to wait around in the corridor and pass the time meditating.

However, Giovanni was a very heavy smoker. The thought of the impossibility of satisfying his craving in these unpolluted precincts filled him with a desperate desire for a cigarette. He walked softly up and down the corridor to distract himself, but without much success. Suddenly, as he turned in the direction of Padre Pio's cell, he was astonished to see a shadowy figure emerging. It was Padre Pio, fully dressed in his habit. To Giovanni's whispered questions and remonstrances he merely said, "Come in here first, and then you can carry out your job in my cell." He led him into the library. "Now then, Giovanni," said he, "have your smoke in here first, and then you can come and attend to me!"

CHAPTER XXXIII

There was another resident who, for a very good reason, never emulated Giovanni Vignolini's spirited dash across the *piazza*. He was blind.

This was Pietruccio. When I went down first, Pietruccio was already an institution, and he became so more and more as the years passed. If he never raced, neither did he ever falter or stumble, for he knew every stone in the place, every step, every obstacle both without and within. He went along at a comfortable gait, greeted by everyone, and naming everyone as he tranquilly returned the greeting. He recognized the voice of practically every single soul.

He tried once—mistakenly, I suppose, or so I should be expected to say—to put his quickness of hearing at the service of the man he worshiped, and got into the most unholy hot water for it. It was during that unhappy visitation during the year of Padre Pio's golden jubilee of his priesthood; a visitation which was an unmerited humiliation for Padre Pio and a source of anger and resentment for those who understood its ridiculousness and injustice.

The monsignor conducting the operation called in for questioning all members of the Community and saw any residents outside who he thought might be helpful or who offered themselves spontaneously. Pietruccio distrusted one of the outside participants in the inquiry and decided to conceal himself in an adjoining room to hear what, under seal of absolute secrecy, was being said.

Alas for his design, he was caught red-handed at his listening post of the adjacent open window; and when the outraged monsignor had finished with him, Pietruccio was a very chastened citizen—or possibly I should say that such he appeared to be; for I cannot help feeling that underneath the outward semblance he would have kept intact that essential, philosophical unflappability which was so characteristic of him.

I should think that blindness is a great producer of philosophy, especially if you have chosen it and are living alongside the man who gave you the choice. Pietruccio, like all those countless others, had come to San Giovanni as a suppliant seeking the cure of his infirmity; and Padre Pio had asked him, "Do you want to have your sight restored or to save your soul?" "If it is a strict choice," said Pietruccio, "I should rather save my soul." "It is a strict choice," replied Padre Pio; and it was a hard and bitter response for a young, strong man.

But Padre Pio did not leave it at that. He kept Pietruccio beside him, and he became an accepted part of the life of the monastery and of all those connected with it. He went on errands for the friars, fetched the post, did anything he could to be helpful. And he was given one great place of honor every morning. He preceded Padre Pio from the sacristy when he came out to say Mass, and he stood beside the altar, with those sightless eyes facing the congregation throughout, except when he knelt at the Consecration.

I do not think anyone would have claimed that

Pietruccio's countenance was cast in an especially spiritual mold. But, with the passage of the years, through the friendship and guidance of Padre Pio and by the daily acceptance of a burden which he knew would never be lifted from him till he died, Pietruccio's face seemed to me during the Mass to have assumed the semblance of a Christian martyr. A strength and an inner light grew within it.

In later years he was joined by another blind lad, much younger than he. The story of this second blind resident of San Giovanni I never heard; but eventually he too shared the place of honor beside the altar at Padre Pio's Mass. They were perhaps an invitation to the rest of the congregation to dwell upon the misfortunes of others, not just upon our own; as well as being an illustration of the fact that sometimes we should accept with resignation certain misfortunes, instead of clamoring for a release which in our blindness we refuse to see as for our ill.

CHAPTER XXXIV

From these residents of San Giovanni, let me now pass to some of those I met there, who came from all over the world, and to some who made the journey down with me.

Think of it. For fifty years they came, literally millions of them, in search of assuagement, courage, or inspiration. None went away empty-handed, even if at first it might sometimes have seemed that way.

That was the case with the ex-spiritualist I met there. At the time of our meeting he was an industrialist in the north of Italy, but when he first heard of Padre Pio he was a young man making his way. In a hotel one evening in a strange town, with nothing to read, he picked up a curious religious book telling of a stigmatist. Idly he glanced through its pages till he fell asleep, and then his busy life took over again.

Nonetheless, the seed had been sown. It remained hidden beneath the turmoil for almost thirty years.

During that time he had become addicted to spiritualism, had introduced his family to it, and one of his sons had become an extraordinarily sensitive medium. Unfortunately this son ended up in a lunatic asylum. His father, then, casting around for assistance in his distraction and remorse, remembered out of the blue the miracle-working stigmatist of whom he had read so long ago; and his subsequent investigations led him one day to San Giovanni Rotondo.

Padre Pio repulsed him brusquely. Before he had had time to tell him the object of his mission, he said to him, "You ruin your son, and then you come running here!" So brusque indeed was the reception he received that his suppliant mood turned to anger, and he left San Giovanni full of rage and resentment. He told me that as he drove up through Italy he vowed that never again would he go near this rough-tongued monk who had treated with such contempt his efforts and his long journey down.

This behavior on the part of Padre Pio was common enough; on numerous occasions he either abruptly refused to confess people or scolded them angrily and sent them packing. This was because he realized that their motives or pleas were superstitious or purely material and egotistical, or that they were treating him like some witch doctor or medicine man and had little thought of reforming their lives. Invariably, so far as my knowledge goes, they were shocked into the reality of things and came back to him in a proper frame of mind. (I think I might here be permitted a brief and humorous illustrative interpolation. It was well known that Padre Pio, in accordance with Our Lady's solemn and specific strictures at Fatima, had very strong views on certain female fashions in dress. When the mini-skirt craze made its impact, no one would dare come to San Giovanni thus clad. But some women who had sought a compromise came down in skirts that were short*ish*. Padre Pio fulminated against these too. So one good compromising lady who had heard of the thunderbolts thought she had better change her skirt before going to confession and borrowed a longer one from a friend. Padre Pio, when her turn came, simply drew back the little shutter, gave her a real good glower, and as he snapped it shut again, said, "Well? Have we been dressing up for carnival, then?")

The rage and resentment of our spiritualist were not very long-lived, and he did come down again. But, as I was able to judge from my conversations with him, he was by nature a stubborn, strongheaded man, and it took quite a time before Padre Pio tamed him. Several times he returned and got little satisfaction from his visits. But one day, after he finished his confession, he had the joy of hearing that his son would be cured; and when I met the father for the first time, his son had not only recovered but become re-established in life and was holding down a position of much responsibility.

To demonstrate of what obdurate stuff the man was made, he told me that during his "post-conversion" period he was standing one day in the little church watching Padre Pio as he sat in the open women's confessional. Several times Padre Pio had looked in his direction as he listened to his penitents, and each time their gaze met our friend lowered his eyes. "After a while," he told me, "I said to myself, But why? Next time I shall keep looking straight at him." So he did. "And," he reminisced, "it was as though two literal flames shot out from those eyes to consume me. By heavens, I tell you, I lowered my gaze in pretty quick time!"

It was Padre Pio's way of teaching him some humility and good manners; which did not prevent him, however, from advising him to use his exuberant temperament when just occasion demanded. He had said he was having trouble with professional Communist agitators among his workers, and he asked, "What shall I do? Shall I take a stick to them?" "My son," replied Padre Pio, "put nails in it!"

CHAPTER XXXV

A very frequent visitor to the slopes of the Gargano was Wilfred Van Singer, an outstanding character whom I had met during the war. The circumstances of that meeting are perhaps also worth narrating.

In the train one day between Bern and Geneva I read in the *Gazette de Lausanne* that a young Italian pilot had flown a fighter plane across the Alps and landed at Lausanne with hardly a drop of fuel left in his tank. The exploit was quite exceptional, because it was midwinter and conditions over the Alps could hardly be described as ideal. I thought the pilot must be a really gritty individual and wondered what had inspired his flight.

Some days later I found out. This same tall, handsome young pilot appeared in my office and, having assured himself of my identity, handed me an urgent plea for assistance from Colonel Montezemolo, the Italian resistance leader in Rome who, most unhappily, was shortly afterward captured and executed.

When, after the war, I told him about Padre Pio, nothing would do but that he accompany me on my next visit, and it became the first of a long series. Padre Pio loved him very much; and many were the occasions when he and his wife were made aware of his presence by an unexpected wave of the perfume.

Wilfred had made me promise that I would let him know any time I was going down to San Gio-

vanni and said that, if humanly possible, he would
drop everything and come too. Once, while in
Rome, I decided on the spur of the moment to slip
down next day for a quick recharging of the batter-
ies and thought that, though there would be no
chance of his making it, I ought, in any case, to let
him know. I sent a telegram apologizing for not in-
forming him in time and promising to remember him
and his family.

Any one who knows the two countries will realize
what it meant to climb into a car at eight o'clock in
the morning in Lausanne (for he had returned there
and settled), drive right across Switzerland and
down the whole Italian peninsula, and arrive at San
Giovanni at eleven o'clock that night. For a man
who by now should have been a sedate businessman
and the responsible father of a family, it was indeed
a remarkable performance. Next day when we met
Padre Pio, I told him not just to give him a blessing
but a sound lecturing as well, because, when he got
into a car, he still confused it with a plane. He
shook his head at him in smiling reproof, and it
struck me that maybe Wilfred had not been alone
when he was admiring the scenery of the winter
Alps. Who could tell with Padre Pio?

He was certainly with his wife and him to give
them comfort and strength when, on a sunny afternoon, their lovely young daughter left them on her
bicycle and in all her youth and innocence was
taken to wait for them where she is now with Padre
Pio, and with that Madonna delle Grazie of whom
her mother shortly before had done so beautiful a
painting.

CHAPTER XXXVI

Wilfred Van Singer had his cross before him when he came down to San Giovanni for the first time. Most people were already bearing one.

Among these were some of the greatest names in Italy, men of whose tragedies I knew personally. Vittorio Cini I also first met in Switzerland. In his heyday he was one of the world's foremost financial and industrial wizards and was the modern Doge of Venice. He had lost his only son, Giorgio, in sad, dramatic circumstances; the son who, as little more than a boy, had gone into Germany where his father was in a prison camp and had managed to free him and get him across the Swiss border. This proud man, who seemed literally to shrink after the death of his son, came down to Padre Pio time after time for comfort and hope, and found the strength to make of the island of San Giorgio, in the Venice lagoon, a home and a vocational training center for nine hundred poor or orphan boys. I went round his workshops of multiple category one day, and visited his training ships, and saw too the vast *palazzo* which he had restored magnificently as a center of international culture; but the brightest moment was when we came across a group of boys trooping out from a schoolroom. As they crowded around him and I saw his eyes light up, I knew that Giorgio had found a lot of younger brothers to help heal his father's heart.

Count Carlo Faina of Perugia, at that time chairman of Italy's largest chemical industry, came to San Giovanni with uppermost in his mind a son who was deaf and dumb. He was one of the most Christian persons I ever met, and his family were exemplary, all bound the more closely together, it was evident, around this afflicted boy. When I introduced Carlo Faina to Padre Pio, he tried to speak but failed. All he could do was weep; and Padre Pio it was who spoke, gently comforting him.

He and his wife took away with them no cure for their son; but they did take away great spiritual solace and understanding, and they spoke always afterward of their gratitude for having met Padre Pio and having heard his unforgettable Mass.

There was a north Italian marquis whom I met purely by chance one evening in the house of the Sanguinettis, and of whom I speak only because of the incidents which happened on the following morning.

We came face to face on a mountain track above the monastery, whither we both had gone, as it transpired, with the same intention. We both wished to collect our thoughts in preparation for a meeting with Padre Pio at which each of us had requests to make of him. Mine, as always, were being formulated mentally beforehand, and I would only ask him verbally to pray in general for my intentions. But the marquis had only one request to make. With an earnestness and supplication that moved me deeply he knelt there and begged him "as the humblest of his servants" that the fatal disease which had struck his wife might be removed from her. It was truly reminiscent of the Gospels.

It is this touching picture that remains engraved in my mind, and what followed is not so clear, but to the best of my recollection Padre Pio said that he would pray for her, and I believe she recovered.

(The words "that he would pray for her" lead me to insert here another short interpolation. How is one to understand or explain the granting of some heartfelt petitions and the refusal of others? Very simply, I think. The alternative responses of Padre Pio, for which I learned to wait and therefrom know immediately what the outcome would be, were substantially either "I shall pray" or "Let us pray for whatever God sees to be best." In their phrasing lies the obvious key.

(I had two good local friends here, a brother and sister, both with young families and therefore with every incentive to wish to live. For the sister, whom I had left in a decline that seemed obviously destined to end in death, I received the first type of answer. It was therefore no surprise when, shortly after my return, on visiting a local golf course, I found her teeing up a ball and saw her hit it straight down the fairway. For her brother, one of the finest doctors this country has ever known, I got the second reply, cabled here by Mrs. Sanguinetti, and I knew, to my sorrow for his family and for all of us, that there was, alas, no recovery for him. He died a week later.)

CHAPTER XXXVII

Last of the Italian friends I want to write about is Alfredo Pizzoni, a man known in his day throughout the length and breadth of Italy.

Alfredo in his youth had spent a year or so in England and was a great admirer of her traditions and institutions as they then were. During the last war he did his duty as a colonel of the famous *Bersaglieri,* and when his troopship was torpedoed *en route* to Africa, possibly with heroic memories of the *Birkenhead* and with better fortune, he lined up his soldiers in proper ranks and got them off in fast, orderly fashion, losing none.

In 1943, when the break with Germany came, he was one of the pioneers of the Italian resistance movement and became underground head of its chief executive organ, the North Italian Committee. That was when I met him.

At the end of the war he became chairman of the Credito Italiano, one of Italy's leading banks, and flung himself into a host of philanthropic activities, heading, for instance, Milan's Red Cross and being a governor of two of the city's hospitals.

I had spoken to him at various times of Padre Pio, and though not a man deeply involved in religion, he had been very much impressed, largely, I imagine, because he knew from past experience that the man he was speaking to was not himself impressed too easily.

He had decided to visit, region by region, all the main branches of his bank and eventually reached Foggia. When he informed the local manager that he intended to go to San Giovanni Rotondo, he was told that appropriate arrangements would be made. "Oh no," said Alfredo, "I am not going there as head of a bank but as an individual pilgrim." So he arrived unannounced like any other normal citizen.

In the course of his stay, while taking a professional look at the hospital, he happened to run into Dr. Sanguinetti and mentioned that he had heard him spoken of by a mutual Scottish friend. The doctor then duly saw to it that he met and spoke with Padre Pio. What passed between them I do not know, but Alfredo fell a happy victim to his influence and stayed that way.

His manner of meeting his death was in harmony with the courage that had characterized his life. He contracted cancer, and I urged him to go to the States, where he had many well-placed friends, but he would not, for two reasons: firstly, because, though he had lived in the world of money, he had stayed a relatively poor man; and secondly, he thought it would be disloyal to go for treatment to a United States clinic when he was so closely identified with the Italian medical scene.

His face and throat were affected, and I can only say that whatever treatment he received had disastrous consequences. This robust, sturdy man was dead in six months, with his face holed and disfigured, and eventually he had suffocated.

He sat in his office right up to the end, I believe in

order that his family might reap the benefit of his dying in harness, conducting the business of the bank with all his usual calm and courtesy. When I visited him, I knew he must be suffering intensely and also subject to embarrassment, but never once did he speak of his illness after he had informed me so stoically of its appearance. All the talk was in normal, ordinary channels, and at the end of our talks he would walk along with me, chatting, to the lift.

One day I called on him on the eve of accompanying my son to a German university. We had our usual talk, and probably he was more relaxed than I could be at the sight of his fantastic self-discipline. We were shaking hands at the lift when he paused in his talk and, with great earnestness, said, "And thank you, old friend, for Padre Pio." Those were the last words I ever heard him speak; when I came back ten days later he was dead.

Strangely, he had never spoken of the possibility of Padre Pio obtaining a cure for him. I don't know why. But he had obviously found something much more important for him at San Giovanni; and Pope Paul VI, then Archbishop of Milan, who gave him the last sacraments, was edified by his demeanor at his last tremendous moment of trial.

"Thank you for Padre Pio." It may seem a tenuous thing on which to hang a chapter. Not at all. The main object of writing this book is that as many people as possible, reading it and turning to him for help and for strength, may be moved in their turn to say, "Thank you, new friend, for Padre Pio."

That would be wonderful, enabling me to give something in return for so very much received.

CHAPTER XXXVIII

A number of men with wealth or high position have appeared in these pages, and I shall later speak of another. Perhaps I should say a word about that before proceeding.

Let us be quite clear that there is nothing admirable about poverty or lack of means unless it is self-imposed. Otherwise we should be extremely foolish to try and abolish it.

Neither is there anything harmful about the just possession of wealth *per se*. It can bring heavy temptations to its owners, and in that respect they are less fortunate than the rest of us. It can also be abused and made a vehicle of exploitation.

But wealth, in the hands of those who see it in perspective and administer it in Christian fashion, can be turned to great advantage, as I have seen done at San Giovanni Rotondo.

I make these remarks lest there should be those who wonder whether the possession of wealth or position obtained favor or privilege at San Giovanni. It did not. Padre Pio saw in the poor the suffering brethren of Christ and loved them the more for that. They were the immense majority of those who came to him. But he likewise had compassion on the rich and powerful, as sons of God, and if they came to him in sincerity for solace or for guidance, they received it, and would at the same time be moved to make better use of their material potential.

He was, however, no respecter of persons, as the following anecdote illustrates.

One nationally and even internationally known political figure who turned up at San Giovanni accompanied by a police motorcycle escort received this welcome from him: "Well, well! How the world has changed since I was young! In those days the police were to be found at the heels of thieves and robbers. Now they go before them on motorcycles to clear the way!"

Hard words; but it appeared clear to those of us who knew of the episode that the man in question had hoped to gain political advantage from the report of his visit, or had come out of vulgar curiosity; and it seems equally clear that the bitter greeting was intended by its shock to reach, if possible, a hardened heart.

CHAPTER XXXIX

The last of those met at San Giovanni to whom I should like to devote a small chapter was not rich in the goods of this world and certainly was not hard of heart.

Every year he appeared there, like the swallows and the almond blossom, and he was just as welcome. Joe Peterson was his name, and he was a postman somewhere in America.

Tall and well built he was and when first he came to see Padre Pio it was in the uniform of a G.I.

Joe, in any kind of gear, would have scared no one; for goodness looked out at you from him. And as that unmistakable figure strode around San Giovanni, one would see him continually receiving a wave or a greeting from the local inhabitants: "Ciao, Joe!"

He spent all his annual vacations visiting Padre Pio, who loved him dearly. But he did not come there merely to receive; he came also to give. Between one holiday and another he devoted a great part of his free time to giving a series of talks and illustrated lectures on San Giovanni in any part of the States where he could fill a hall; and each year the proceeds were duly brought to Padre Pio for his hospital. In other words, he spread the good news, and he gave those who heard it the opportunity of participating in the good work.

CHAPTER XL

Scotland too took her stance at San Giovanni, not only in the present writer, but through much better men.

Some of the very happiest years of my life had been spent at the Scots College, Rome; and certainly the four most profitable years were those passed in the lecture halls of Rome's Gregorian University, which the Scots students attended.

Padre Pio knew of my having been at Scots, and already he had had visits from Monsignor Clapperton of Aberdeen, the old rector, and from Monsignor Flanagan of Glasgow, the present one. When I told him in his cell one day that my old rector was waiting in the corridor, he raised his eyes to heaven in mock horror and said, "A rector! God save us from all such!" Recognizing them for the fine types they were, he treated both of them with great consideration and warmth.

While I was there once, Monsignor Clapperton brought down with him Monsignor "Gerry" Rogers of Glasgow, once my gay, carefree fellow student and now a member of the Sacra Romana Rota.

The next evening in the parlor there was talk of Scotland. Monsignor Rogers and I had an old friend who was a somewhat colorful parish priest there of whom we spoke, and I then got him to repeat a tale concerning the priest which he had recounted around the fire the previous night.

This stout pastor had been awakened in the middle of the night by a very worried young curate. The curate had received a message that there was a dying woman who was in need of his ministrations; but when he went to the house a burly non-Catholic husband told him in no uncertain language that he was having no unprintable priest in there and slammed the door. "I see," said our friend. "Have you the Blessed Sacrament with you?" "Yes." "Good, I'll go back there along with you."

When they returned, an irate husband, opening the door once more, shouted, "I told you . . ." which was just as far as he got, because he then found himself flat on his back. "Go ahead now with what you have to do, Father," said this splendid example of the Church militant, "and I shall take care of our friend." He did, very adequately, and so his "friend's" wife was enabled to die with the comforts of her religion.

Padre Pio and the others laughed. And then Padre Pio remarked, "You know, as a young priest I too had to use some unorthodox pressure to be able to administer the last sacraments." We all looked at him in surprise. "No, no, not that kind of pressure," he smiled.

"I was young and at my wits' end," he said. "I was attending a sick man who, the doctor told me, would not last the night. But when I suggested to him, trying not to alarm him unduly, that it would be a good idea for me to hear his confession, there was no way he could be persuaded. I tried everything. There was nothing to be done. He would confess, he told me, when he felt better. Well, I thought, desperate cases need desperate remedies. So I got up, went toward the door, and said, 'In that case, then, good-by. We shall meet again at the cemetery.' 'What?' cried the sick man, suddenly galvanized. 'What do you mean?' 'Alas, my poor friend, the doctor has spoken to me, and he assures me you will not see morning!' (He shook his head reminiscently.) "*Then,* then indeed you should have seen the change! He did confess, received Holy Communion most devoutly, knowing it to be his last, and he died with composure and resignation."

I was reminded of a lovely phrase Padre Pio had used some time previously. An Italian professor, who was a member of the Hospital Committee, had brought his little son with him to receive his first Holy Communion, and after Mass the child had gone to Padre Pio to thank him. "There now," he said, as he patted the boy on the head. "God bless you. And may your *last* Holy Communion be even purer than your first!"

CHAPTER XLI

And Ireland? What of the country of my origins and present adoption? Ireland has traveled far toward Padre Pio since that day when Dr. Sanguinetti told me no one ever came from here and showed me the one solitary letter that had ever arrived from Ireland, sent by a woman in Derry.

But Padre Pio did not wait for people to begin coming from here to him; he first made the trip himself; not in visible bi-location, but manifesting his presence with his perfume. He admitted as much when I saw him shortly afterward, during one of my earliest visits.

It happened during a six weeks' absence from Ireland. My wife had written me a letter concerning a family matter which was worrying her deeply. She had not had time for a reply when, one evening as she was sitting nursing her anxiety, she became aware that the room was full of a beautiful perfume. She was astounded and, like the American woman in her San Giovanni hotel, she searched around to see whether a bottle of perfume had spilled or been broken. There was no trace of any bottle, broken or otherwise; and then all at once it struck her what it must be. Padre Pio had come to comfort her and to let her know that all would be well, as indeed so it proved. She was greatly moved, as can be imagined; and she told me that she prayed as she stood there breathing in that wonderful perfume until, after several minutes, it disappeared as inexplicably as it had come.

Naturally she thought that by then I had already been to San Giovanni and had spoken of the matter to Padre Pio. But I had not, and received her second letter with the account of her extraordinary experience on the eve of my departure for there from Milan.

Companion of the trip was the man who had brought me down there first of all, Piero Pellizzari of Genoa. During the journey I told him of my wife's experience, one which, as I was aware, was not new either to him or to his wife. But it was not part of my program to speak of it to Padre Pio, whom I did not then know very well.

However during our second and last brief talk with him, Piero asked his prayers for quite a lengthy and detailed list of intentions, the last of which I felt were added on the spur of the moment in order to keep him with us longer, before he passed to the next group. Finally, to my great embarrassment, in a last effort to detain him, he blurted out: "And, Padre, the Signora McCaffery, in Ireland, felt a strange odor!" It was a *gauche* and laughable phrase, which he had used under the pressure of thinking up something else, and Padre Pio laughed and repeated it with jesting irony: *"Uno strano odore?"* he asked. And then, turning toward me, he said very gently, "Even beyond the sea?"

This episode was for me the first link between Padre Pio and Ireland. It was, however, still something "within the family," and the fact that I had heard Padre Pio's Mass for the first time on St. Patrick's morning seemed to me a pointer indicating the desirability of a link, not on a family but on a national scale. I began to preach the gospel of San Giovanni to friends and acquaintances who seemed apt material.

There is a well-known stretch of road hugging the coast between Donegal Town and the little fishing port of Killybegs. A song has rightly been written about it. I used to call it Padre Pio's first Irish parish, because at either end of it and in the middle dwelt the first people who had gone down from Ireland (so far as I know) to San Giovanni: Group Captain Nicolas Tindal and his wife; Peter Folan, man of many parts; and ourselves.

Next people to go down there were Dr. Jack O'Doherty and his wife and family, from Dublin. They went all the way by car and had an introduction to Dr. Sanguinetti so that he might present them personally to Padre Pio. But the O'Dohertys are exceptional people; and, after seeing him say Mass on one of his bad mornings, they decided they would not add to his burdens, did not approach the doctor, and were happy just to be there.

Afterward I recounted this to Padre Pio, and he replied, "That was very wrong of them. I should like to have seen them. Tell them that in this life one must be like a grandfather clock and have a face of brass!" Needless to say, he knew they were there and appreciated their courtesy and sensitivity; and he has repaid them for it many times since.

However, speaking to friends was not enough. After much soul-wrestling I decided that a talk over Radio Eireann would be the thing to go for. The soul-wrestling was because I knew that if ever I gave such a talk I was putting myself up as an Aunt Sally. If I was ever seen thereafter with an alcoholic beverage in my hand, or heard to apostrophize picturesquely man or beast, someone would be sure to say, "There's the holy man for ye!" It's a grand old Irish custom.

But Padre Pio was worth that and a great deal more, and a script was presented to Radio Eireann. One of their officials received me kindly and said that they wanted very much to have the talk but there was one difficulty which would have to be overcome. The formidable Archbishop of Dublin, John Charles McQuaid, always liked to be consulted before any specifically Catholic program was put on the air. If there was a talk on such a thing as a miracle-working stigmatist without his approval being sought, the least they could expect was excommunication!

Now "John Charles," as he was commonly called, was a great and admirable cleric, but of the ivory tower variety, and I had long presumptuously desired to cross swords with him on one or two matters where it seemed to me his policies were mistaken. This was a chance to kill two birds with one stone, and so, for the purpose of obtaining a proper introduction, I went to see our own Bishop of Raphoe, that kind and holy man, Dr. McNeely, whom I knew well.

In the course of having tea with him I brought up the subject of the script and asked him would he care, informally and unofficially, to vet it. He shied away at once, but I produced it, insisting that I was not looking for an *imprimatur* but only for a frank and confidential personal opinion, and handed it over to him, suggesting he peruse it while we sipped our tea. He took it with as much enthusiasm as if he was being handed a dangerous viper.

However, to my delight, as he read it his demeanor changed completely, and at the end he was even enthusiastic. "This," said he, "can only do good. It is factual and restrained and orthodox, and it concerns an obviously saintly man."

I then asked him for an introduction to the archbishop for the purpose I had in mind; but poor Dr. McNeely balked at that, for "John Charles" was "a hard man," and who knew what might be his reaction to having this wild and woolly character landed on his doorstep? "No," said he, "I'll do better. I'll take the matter up with him myself when we are at the bishops' meeting this month." My heart sank with foreboding, for the bishop was a gentle soul; but naturally all I could do was to thank him profusely.

Our next meeting took place at the Letterkenny Horse and Cattle Show, the bishop being an ardent breeder of the native shorthorn cattle. He confessed to me that he had been shot down in flames. "John Charles" had not seen "that a talk on Padre Pio would be of any great advantage to the Irish people." I don't hold it against him, for there was so much that was good in him and in his episcopal activities; but I am very sorry indeed that we did not have the matter out.

Being of a pigheaded disposition, I kept that script against eventualities, and I intend to print it later in the book, because I think that "John Charles" would now agree with me, and also that it might still be of benefit, not only to Irish people but to any who happen to read it anywhere.

"John Charles's" rejection was probably providential; for in casting around, I came up with something much better: an article in the national press by the Jesuit writer, Father Robert Nash. His books and the splendid series of articles which have been published by a national newspaper for around thirty years have done as much for the lay Catholics of Ireland as have his equally long series of spiritual retreats for religious.

I happened to speak to him about Padre Pio just as he was about to set out for Rome, and during his stay there he found time to go down to San Giovanni Rotondo. It was the *coup de foudre*. Just as a painter sees more in a painting, or an engineer in delicate machinery, than do the rest of us uninstructed mortals, so did Father Nash realize infinitely more than the rest of us what spiritual altitudes Padre Pio had attained. He spoke with him, witnessed his whole day, and served his Mass; and when he came back he wrote an article entitled "Padre Pio" which started a stream of pilgrims going down from Ireland which has continued and grown to this day.

Those of his readers who could not make the journey became much interested in Padre Pio, and since the Mercier Press had published Malachy Carroll's book, also entitled *Padre Pio,* about the same time, they were able to learn a great deal more.

The enthusiastic travelers, too, who came back from San Giovanni spread the good tidings all around them. English translations of lives of Padre Pio began to appear. The BBC did a splendid documentary on him which Radio Telefis Eireann carried more than once. Since the death of Padre Pio devoted people have led organized pilgrimages to San Giovanni and instituted prayer groups. Miss Mairead Doyle, who was one of the first Irish pilgrims I met at San Giovanni when the stream began, has been outstanding in these activities and has lectured and shown the BBC film, as well as two others, all over Ireland. Another Irishwoman, Miss Mary Ingoldsby, who last year went to live permanently in San Giovanni, is translating the volume of Padre Pio's letters, *L'Epistolario,* into English. And, of course, the lone letterwriter from Derry has now had a host of followers. All in all, today knowledge of and attachment to Padre Pio is so widespread among the Irish people as to stand comparison with those of any other country outside his native Italy.

If we let him do it, I still believe that Padre Pio has a special mission to accomplish for Ireland.

Ireland has her saints; no nation has more, or greater ones. But they did not all stay at home. They brought the faith to the ends of the earth, and they became saints of Italy, France, Germany, Switzerland, and in latter centuries of the whole English-speaking world and of what are now termed the "emerging" countries. Maybe she in her turn can afford now to adopt a saint, one of the greatest the Church has ever produced, a man of our own times; and as well as that, at a moment when many bishops, priests, and religious have been afflicted by a spiritual palsy, one of the most exemplary priests and religious the world has ever seen.

CHAPTER XLII

I want to say a word about some people I met, not at San Giovanni but elsewhere, because of their connection with Padre Pio.

As in the case of Elena Bandini, I met Mario Sanvico on what proved to be his deathbed. He was a small industrialist of Perugia, and together with Dr. Sanguinetti and the Marquis Sacchetti of Rome had formed the nucleus of the first Hospital Committee. When Dr. Sanguinetti died, and there were so many eager candidates for the succession, it was not easy, as I have said, for Padre Pio to reject those people who, whatever their inappropriateness for the post, looked to him as a spiritual father. So, with holy guile, when he had agreed that Gino Ghisleri was the man for the job, he asked me to take him to Perugia and Rome, tell Giovanni Sacchetti and Mario Sanvico what he wanted, and have the appointment formally made and rendered public by them.

I had never met either, and first had to introduce myself and explain the situation, before bringing on the selected candidate.

Giovanni Sacchetti was head of one of the oldest noble families in Italy, a hereditary holder of high office at the Vatican, chairman of a much-respected private Roman bank, and one of the pleasantest, most kindhearted, most unostentatious persons it has ever been my good luck to meet. He wore his distinctions unobtrusively, almost with shyness; and few people were more loyal or devoted to Padre Pio than he. The meeting with him was most civilized and friendly.

That with Mario Sanvico would be hard to forget; I can still see that emaciated face on the pillow and the eyes bright with fever which lit up when I told him why I was there. Summoning up his energy, he raised himself on his elbow and exclaimed: "Well done! God bless you. You see, from all parts they flock to Padre Pio—all looking for something, begging for favors, leaning on him, and few of them *pitying* him!"

Looking at him there, he too dying of a painful cancer, I thought: Yes, *you* are thinking of him but, unlike me, in a big way. Here was a man who had toiled and labored for the creation of the hospital, Padre Pio's dream; who for years had been his friend and confidant. He was not old. Surely he might have asked Padre Pio for the favor of being healed—as for instance the present writer had done so often. But Mario Sanvico was of better stuff than that and had become a saint. His exclamation of pleasure for the very small effort I was making sprang from a man who was willingly accepting suffering and death for one whom he recognized as chosen by God for a mission great enough to merit such a sacrifice.

This world of Padre Pio was one that pierced in various ways, according to one's capacity, the ephemeral camouflage of a brief, transient existence and put it into the true perspective of eternity.

CHAPTER XLIII

The man I next tell of was perhaps the most complex character I ever came across in that world.

Emanuele Brunatto was his name. He was expert in many fields: finance, industry, politics, literature, the cinema, and—most importantly—he knew his way around the Vatican. When I first heard him spoken of, he was living in Paris; but he was southern Italian, and he was the earliest disciple of Padre Pio of all those that I met. In the religious works which he published, he signed himself "The Publican"; and from what he told me, it seemed he had been a great sinner in his youth, was converted by Padre Pio, and to make a solid job of the conversion he stayed close to him for a year or so before he betook himself back to the world outside. He even went to Pietralcina and stayed with Padre Pio's parents, the more to identify himself with him. This was typical of the man, for he was a most determined character, and whatever he decided to do, he did with all his might.

When the idea of the hospital was first mooted, his was the first really large subscription which enabled it to get off the ground. But important as this was, he had another achievement to his previous credit which far outweighed it. His was the final push which freed Padre Pio from his years of "imprisonment."

I have already referred to the Church's well-justified caution on living "saints." Especially does she distrust mass manifestations of emotional fervor by people unpracticed in discernment and therefore wide open to error and to superstition. In the course of her long history she has become familiar with cases of delusion, autosuggestion, and even diabolical possession, precisely in the stigmatic field.

Just imagine, therefore, the distrust and skepticism with which reports of a stigmatist appearing in the backward Gargano region were received in Rome.

When I met Padre Pio, one could say that he had won his direct conflicts with the Devil: those terrible struggles in which he took even brutal physical punishment from him, and which one will find documented in his early letters to his spiritual adviser. Indeed the Devil himself confessed his complete defeat. An English Capuchin gave me an account of an exorcism he had witnessed at Loreto. The evil spirit, who spoke in tongues, said bitterly that he could do nothing with "that man at San Giovanni Rotondo" but, with malicious pleasure, that he could still work havoc among those in contact with him.

He was as good as his word, and he worked through others to shackle this most powerful enemy who would so hinder and defeat his designs. There took place, as is well known, a dreadful period for Padre Pio, lasting from the early twenties to the early thirties, a prolonged night of the soul during which he was forbidden public contact: no confessions, no public Mass, not even epistolary contact with the faithful. He was scorned, ridiculed, and subjected to interminable interrogations. He was also subjected to a series of humiliating medical examinations. His transfer from San Giovanni to another region of Italy was prevented only because the local populace took measures to resist it by force, and it was foreseen that any attempt at police intervention was liable to provoke bloodshed.

Emissaries came from Rome and elsewhere to study him, generally biased and prejudiced against him. Among them was Father Agostino Gemelli, founder of Milan's Catholic University and a close friend of the reigning Pope, Pius XI. Father Gemelli came quite convinced that he was going to find a hoaxer or a mental case, and in his approach to Padre Pio he was brusque and peremptory. He demanded to be shown his wounds. Padre Pio, whose spiritual sensibility and natural reserve had been outraged by all the furor and crude impositions to which he had had to submit, told him (correctly) that if he could produce written authority for such an examination he was willing to undergo it, but otherwise no. Father Gemelli, a strong character used to getting his own way, returned to Rome and produced a report confirming the wisdom of the segregation.

But Pius XI must also have received, in the course of the years in question, positive reports on Padre Pio, and if he was aware of it, he must have been especially impressed by the wholly favorable report by Dr. Festa, the competent physician to whom the Capuchin General had eventually exclusively confided the medical investigations of the stigmata. From being cynical and even contemptuous of the whole business at the beginning, this man became one of Padre Pio's devoted disciples. He wrote a book which included a meticulous account of the experiments carried out to test every possible hypothesis based on humanly explicable causation. He ended it with a humble profession of faith and the logical deduction that there was only one possible explanation, that of benign superhuman intervention.

However, whatever stage the Pope's thinking had reached, when Emanuele Brunatto decided to take action and do us all a tremendous favor, Padre Pio was still "the prisoner of San Giovanni." The Vatican was still either not wholly convinced or was unwilling to appear to give approval to something which might spark off a popular eruption, with consequences that were unforeseeable.

Emanuele moved, as always, with intelligence and decision. He marshaled his contacts, prepared his attack, bearded the lion in his den, and took the Vatican by storm. With a man of Pius XI's stern character on the throne, this was no mean feat.

The main arguments he must have used are perhaps not hard to imagine. To prevent a man so clearly marked by God from accomplishing his mission was assuredly to fly in the face of Providence; and besides, during these years of trial, Padre Pio had been a shining example of total submission to the will of his superiors. In face of all the evidence, a man with the intelligence of Pius XI must have been convinced of the authenticity of Padre Pio's sanctity and stigmata, and the only objection left would be that of prudence. But it was Emanuele Brunatto who gave that decisive push, and through him Padre Pio was at last set free.

Many years later Emanuele gave a repeat performance, and it was then that I met him personally.

The Devil had again given proof of his ability to wreak havoc *around* Padre Pio, and there were jealousies, resentments, and oppositions both in the milieu of San Giovanni and within the Capuchin Order itself. Negative reports found their way again to the corridors of power in Rome, and these were fanned by the sensation-mongering articles of anti-Catholic foreign journalists who made a meal of the emotion they found in the south. It began to be said that things were out of hand at San Giovanni and that, Padre Pio or not, discipline had to be restored and superstition suppressed. A full-scale apostolic visitation was ordered, and a Roman monsignor was given the job.

The visitation was given full publicity, once more to the hurt and humiliation of Padre Pio, and the whole world press had stories on it. I read about it in an Irish newspaper during my summer vacation; and on returning to Italy, I called on the monsignor, then passing some days in Rome, on my way down to San Giovanni.

The interview was somewhat hectic. When, in one outburst, I told him that Padre Pio was a beacon light for the entire world, he replied scornfully, "A beacon light! At least two hundred people have written using that term!" I asked him whether he did not find that a proof of what I was saying. He told me that some of the happenings at San Giovanni were infantile; for instance, what follows:

A custom had grown up that in the evening people would gather at a point above the monastery where they could see the window of Padre Pio's cell, and they would sing hymns as a way of saying good night to him. As he left his cell, he would wave to them and give them his blessing. The monsignor told me that two men had been seen to quarrel, each saying that Padre Pio had been waving to him personally. I asked him whether it was not better that they should quarrel childishly over that than less childishly over wine, women, or playing cards; and I informed him that, if he considered it well, Padre Pio *was* waving personally to each person in the crowd.

The monsignor was a good man, perhaps blinkered by ecclesiastical bureaucracy. He shamed me by calming down and smilingly asking me to pray that he would do his job well and present a good report. I never met him again, but someone told me that he too had eventually fallen under the spell of the man he had been investigating, as I know happened later on to Father Gemelli.

Next day I met Padre Pio and got a large, welcoming embrace from him. "Padre," I exclaimed forthwith, "my wife and I read the news in Ireland. What a rotten business for you! What a present Providence has sent you for the year of your golden jubilee of the priesthood!" "Eh!" he replied with feeling. "Just exactly for my golden jubilee!" I gave him what might be termed an upstart, impudent grin and said, "Well, Padre, you *did* ask to suffer, didn't you?" He drew back a little and then, using a phrase in dialect, said: "And so, your advice is to try out this one too?" "Yes, Padre!" He laughed delightedly, bestowed another embrace upon me, and said, "Now *you* understand what it is all about!"

Maybe, but that afternoon Gino Ghisleri told me that the old warrior, Emanuele Brunatto, was about to take to the arena again and wanted him to come and discuss the situation with him in Paris. Would I come too? I had a backlog of work to get through, but we arranged a halfway meeting at Grenoble. It took place in the Trois Dauphins hotel, where we found Emanuele had engaged a conference room and had his most efficient personal secretary present to take the minutes of the conference.

He opened the proceedings by looking at us and saying very naturally, "Gentlemen, before we begin our talks, I take it that we all realize we are not alone here." He was merely expressing what the other two of us felt sure about, that Padre Pio was with us, but it was his actual saying of it and his manner that were striking—as if he were giving a normal introduction to an ordinary board meeting.

It was altogether a memorable day, during which the situation at San Giovanni was thoroughly examined, proposals made and discussed, and decisions taken. That may sound presumptuous. It was not. The presumption was all on the part of those who refused to see the grandiose thing that God had put before their noses.

We also discussed a planned collaboration on a wider spectrum of religious activities, including the use of newspapers and the setting up of a film unit. We did achieve some collaboration in the fields of press and cinema for some time, until Emanuele's death, but all was done by telephone and correspondence, we never met again. I was fascinated by Emanuele Brunatto's deep intelligence and strength of will, both of which qualities he now proceeded to demonstrate once more in defense of Padre Pio.

He mounted a campaign of very steely correspondence with the Vatican, he again marshaled his wide contacts, and he prepared and printed a large and detailed publication which, had it been circulated, would most certainly have given effect to his threat of creating an international scandal.

I cannot with certainty give the reasons which led to the visitation's being allowed to die a natural death. They could have been several and varied; but I feel there is no doubt that Emanuele Brunatto again played great part in ensuring that the graces which had been vouchsafed to Padre Pio would be made as freely available to others as God and His servant wished.

CHAPTER XLIV

It has just struck me that there may be readers who, conditioned to look askance either at alleged manifestations of the Devil or at his very existence, may marvel at the ease with which he and his manifestations were referred to in the preceding chapter. I remember a missionary saying that in the world of Western civilization we had a lack of awareness of Satan, because long centuries of Christianity had, as it were, constrained him to stay in the background; but that he had visited spots where a Christian foot had never before trodden, and the presence of Satan there was really palpable to him.

At San Giovanni not only the presence of God but that of Satan too, in his fury against this citadel, was sometimes revealed. I only met people there who were under his influence in, let us say, a normal evil kind of way. I was never present or spoke with anyone who had assisted at the scenes of people brought down for exorcism. I read of them. But two Milanese doctors who had just returned from their first visit told me they had had a blood-curdling experience.

It was summer, and Padre Pio was saying his Mass in the open air. Some poor girl subject to demoniac possession had either been taken down there or had made her own way. During the Mass she appeared on the balcony of one of the houses below the *piazza* and began to call out foul abuse and obscenities at Padre Pio. The doctors said it was clear to them that, rather than her being prompted, there was someone else speaking through her. They told me that Padre Pio, deathly pale, continued uninterruptedly to say Mass, and that eventually the girl retired from the balcony, with what later sequel I never heard.

I asked one of the doctors why they had taken no steps to have the girl removed. He said that he and the rest of the people present were rooted to the ground, that it was absolutely spine-chilling. Not a soul spoke or moved.

CHAPTER XLV

What of the other members of the monastery Community at San Giovanni Rotondo?

As I ask the question, I see a whole series of faces rise before me; and first and foremost that of Padre Agostino.

A strong face it was, ruddy of complexion, with a snow-white beard. He was crippled with rheumatism when I knew him, already a background figure, from whom one received a smile and a courteous nod as he moved slowly along the first-floor monastery corridor. Everybody paid him the greatest respect. He had several times been Father Guardian during Padre Pio's fifty-year sojourn, and for a great many years he had been his confessor.

In his cell one evening I saw Padre Pio in a completely new light. I had been strolling along with him toward his own cell when he stopped and asked me if I should like to pay a visit to Padre Agostino, who was confined to bed.

Padre Pio sat on the bed to chat to him; he seemed completely relaxed; and as they talked of events of the day and commented on them, I suddenly saw him as one very nice and humorous old man talking to another.

Padre Pio in all the years of his monastic life never held the post of Father Guardian. During the time I knew him he was spiritual director to the Community, and the other friars often addressed him by the title of Padre Spirituale. I met a succession of Guardians, some pleasant and retiring, one vain—who did not last long—one rigid and severe, nicknamed "The Jailer," one devoted to Padre Pio like a prefect to his headmaster, and then there was Padre Carmelo da Sessano.

There was a man. He had been trained as an archivist and saw that Padre Pio's letters were collected and put safely away. He it was who had the imagination to arrange that the Mass said in front of the hospital be discreetly filmed in color that it might be there for posterity.

He was the ideal Father Guardian for that unique monastery. First of all, he realized to the full who and what Padre Pio was, and he did everything possible to facilitate his mission. The Community, the lay collaborators, and the pilgrims who flowed around and through the monastery every day, all of them he supervised with an easy competence. His reactions were quick-fire; and he had a very fine sense of humor.

Above all he was intelligent, and it was a pleasure to converse with him. But once you had gained his confidence, he could display the enthusiasms and ingenuousness of a boy.

He conceived, for instance, the idea of quietly registering Padre Pio's conversations with him and his fellow friars when they were gathered together, or his evening talks with friends and collaborators in the parlor. "Just imagine," he said, "if we had tapes of St. Francis and St. Anthony today! What a wonderful story it would be for us all! Well, let us give future generations the benefit of this great saint we have here."

(In those days, these were strong words for a Superior to use; but Padre Carmelo disdained tempering conviction with exaggerated prudence. He waved his hand once at a row of files in his cell and averred: "The world will be amazed beyond words when the contents of these correspondence dossiers are revealed." That was another proof of his ingenuousness. He thought the world would be as intelligent or in good faith as he was.)

On the question of the tapes, he kept after Gino Ghisleri and myself, urging us to get him the kind of microphone-recorder that he could wear slung around his neck under his habit. I do not know where he had heard or read of this, but he was quite convinced that men as knowledgeable of the outside world as we were would have no difficulty in laying hands on one. Today it would have been easy. Then the science of electronics was in its infancy, and we did not know how or where to look.

His tenacity got results; in desperation, Gino did manage to unearth exactly the thing he was looking for. His delight was phenomenal; and we left him poised for putting posterity once more in his debt.

Next time we saw him the gadget was not even mentioned. Tactfully, we asked him how the recording was going. He flushed a little sheepishly and said, "Sorry, it's a fiasco." "Why?" "H'mph!" he replied. "When I switch on, *he* switches off! Each time I have set the machine in motion, he has immediately gone mute!"

Gino and I laughed till the tears came. "What?" we asked him. "Can you believe all that you do about Padre Pio and imagine he could be taken in by a microphone under a habit?" To console him, we offered to let him try it out on us.

Padre Onorato is a friar in a category all by himself. During all the years that I went to San Giovanni, on all the occasions on which I sat in the group surrounding Padre Pio, in parlor, porch, small terrace, or in the garden, Padre Onorato was seated alongside him. He totally revered Padre Pio and was his faithful shadow. In the conversations, he would follow all the speakers with keen interest but only occasionally fill in a pause with a question or observation.

In pictures of Padre Pio saying High Mass, giving Benediction, or participating in other ceremonies, the man most often at his side is Padre Onorato.

He is small, dark, with well-defined features and two intelligent, controlled brown eyes. Only slowly across the years did I get to know him well. Since the death of Padre Pio I have corresponded with him regularly. He has traveled much since then, filling up the great void in his life by lecturing both in Italy and abroad on the man whom he loved and loves so well. He never passed through Milan without calling for a talk over old times, and today he never misses visiting my son there.

What I am going to say now would surprise Padre Onorato exceedingly. He is possibly the most unselfish man I have ever known, apart from the man he so admired. Priests and religious, despite their dedication, remain human beings; and where men and women lead cloistered lives, the chief temptations are to jealousy and vanity, even, and perhaps especially, over trivial things. Here was a man constantly by the side of someone to whom people came

from every corner of the earth. It would have been
so easy and natural to acquire a sense of primacy
among his brethren, to be jealous if someone else
seemed to be preferred. All the time there were
friars and lay people who appeared to take precedence in the attentions or even the fatherly affection
of Padre Pio. But when Padre Pio showed anyone
respect or affection, they automatically received it
with wholehearted sincerity from Padre Onorato
too. He was content to be there, to be alongside, to
be *sempre a disposizione*.

Padre Giacomo was wholly contained, completely
unflappable, unemotional in his appearance, but with
a heart as big as St. Peter's. Among his official
duties was that of being French correspondent for
the monastery, and he had a heavy mail to look
after. He also interviewed and helped any French-
speaking visitors. But he will always be remembered
by me, and by a multitude of other people, as the
unofficial or semi-official photographer attached to
Padre Pio. He accepted all the gruff or ironical comments that his generally unwilling subject ever gave
him, the jokes, the vetoes; but he kept on, and he
has provided the future generations beloved of
Padre Carmelo, not with a set of formal photographs, but with glimpses of Padre Pio at work, at
prayer, and in his informal contacts with other
members of the Community and with a variety of
visitors.

I said that even if I wanted to I could never forget
Padre Pio for long, because as well as in Ciccone's
portrait in the study, he is present photographically
in practically every room in the house. For the same

reason, I could never forget Padre Giacomo, the creator of so mush pleasure and inspiration.

Of Father Dominic, the American friar, I have already spoken. He was one of my first "guardian angels" to ensure entrance to the monastery, for it was natural that I should ask to see the English-speaking member of the Community. But Father Dominic knew well that on these occasions I was not using his friendship only to breach the monastery walls; I very much wanted to see and speak with him too.

He came of well-established German immigrant stock, who had brought with them and kept that exemplary piety which was to be found in Germany, especially in Bavaria and in the Rhineland. In the circle of his family and his immediate relatives in the United States there had been a heavy crop of religious vocations; and one of his cousins became Bishop of Chicago.

If I was asked to name his chief qualities, I would say his sanctity, his simplicity of soul, and his compassionate understanding for his fellow man.

Though we had both identified extensively with the Italian scene through long years of residence there, there was something very pleasant and relaxing in being able to chat in English in his cell and discuss things from a broadly common background.

I have a memory of the evening of an oppressive day in early summer. As Padre Pio arrived on the terrace he drew a deep breath and said, half to himself, "Finally, after twenty-four hours, a breath of air!"

He then took a notion to display interest in my past and background. "Go on," he said, "you are no Scotsman. Anyone who laughs as you do can only

be a Neapolitan!" And then: "You are the eternal
wanderer. I don't suppose—well, I mean since your
boyhood—you have spent more than seven years at
a stretch in any one country!" (Curious to know
why he had used a number like seven instead of the
more normal five or ten, I checked afterward. He
was correct.)

In the midst of the talk, suddenly Father Dominic
appeared on the terrace, wearing that charming, in-
fectious smile of his. He had been in the States for a
visit to his family, and everyone, Padre Pio first of
all, gave him a great welcome.

When he turned to greet me, we naturally spoke
for some minutes in English, and I can still see
plainly the interest and pleasure in Padre Pio's eyes
as he looked from one to the other as we talked, obviously enjoying with the rest the sound of a foreign
tongue being spoken on this remote little Italian
monastery terrace by two of his spiritual sons.

Father Dominic did not die at San Giovanni; his
last days there were shadowed by being drawn
through obedience into one of those distressing
investigations—this time, alas, decreed by an American General of the Order—which so afflicted and hu-
miliated Padre Pio. He left the monastery an unhappy, grief-stricken man.

But of one thing I am certain. Wherever and however he died in the States, he too was certainly
helped over the stile by his beloved Padre Pio.

Since humor and piety and pathos were often in-
termingled at San Giovanni, let me insert here a tale
that is relevant, though not regarding any of the
Community.

It concerns Gino Ghisleri who, sage constructer

as he was of roads, tunnels, and bridges, was looking ahead to the end of his own road, or tunnel, and wanted to make sure it would come out in the right place. "Padre," said he, "if you die before me, you *will* pull me into heaven, won't you, even if by the hair of the head?" Padre Pio gave a glance at the said head and answered, "Your hair, it seems to me, is pretty thin. I fear it would have to be by the scruff of the neck!"

Talk of heaven is a fitting introduction to Padre Mariano. Though small of stature, like Goldsmith's parson he pierced the clouds and "eternal sunshine settled on his head."

After ordination, his principal studies had been on the Church's great ascetics, and these studies had certainly had their effect upon him and on his spiritual make-up. His spirituality was indeed deep, sterner than that of his brethren; but there was always an underlying softness in his nature which made him quick to understanding and compassion. He made an ideal chaplain for the hospital.

I could go on for reams talking of the members of that Community: Padre Vincenzo, the ruddy-faced Father Porter who sat at his little window giving onto the entrance corridor, listening to the tales of all those who had a special reason for wanting to see Padre Pio personally, and who also kept the confession register; Padre Giambattista di S. Elia, that quiet man whose sanctity was sustained and freshened by a deep sense of humor; Padre Tarcisio, the mighty Friar Tuck who cleft the crowds to make way for Padre Pio and protected him from the onslaughts of their enthusiasm; Padre Ermelindo, who spent some time in the Capuchin monastery away up in the northern fastnesses of Donegal; the little brother from strife-torn Trieste, sweeping the corridors and doing other menial tasks with cheerful word and smile; the quiet, youthful monastery cook, who ensured that no calorie-calculators were ever required as a result of his labors; "Brother Bill," that quiet American who arrived during the last years of Padre Pio's life, and who worked to such purpose that he is now "Father Bill," though the name he has taken in religion is that of Joseph Pius or, more connotationally in Italian, Padre Giuseppe Pio; there was the little old brother, lame and bent double, who spoke to no one as he hobbled along, but who, when he met Padre Pio, would silently stoop to grasp his hand and kiss it.

Throughout my years of visiting San Giovanni, there was a whole procession of friars whose faces I remember with warmth but whose names, like those of many lay collaborators, I never knew or unhappily have forgotten. Old and young, venerable or full of promise, and all called to a very rewarding but most demanding tenor of life; all of them blessed by the example and guidance of Padre Pio, but each constrained to a very subordinate role, that of being viewed only or chiefly in the reflected light of someone else. There was ample occasion for the Devil to tempt them to vanity or resentment, but I cannot recall witnessing a single instance of it. Holy men, patient men, charming men they were, and, as they realized, above all fortunate men.

Of two members of the Community I must write in a manner so special that it will take two further chapters.

CHAPTER XLVI

Padre Eusebio, like St. John with Our Lord, was the disciple whom Padre Pio loved.

The finest photograph ever to come out of San Giovanni Rotondo was that of these two greeting each other after Padre Eusebio had been absent for some time from the monastery. The camera caught wonderfully the fatherly pleasure and affection on the face of one and the confident, filially affectionate, returning gaze of the other.

I spoke of Padre Pio's refusal to be consoled after the death of Dr. Sanguinetti, and of how Giovanni Vignolini, his infirmarian, had been, as it were, swamped by the hospital. This was a period of desolation for him. Not everyone had the delicacy of texture which would persuade him to let them attend to those wounds of which he was so shy and sensitive. Nor was there now anyone on whom he felt he could wholly lean at times, to whom he could open his heart and be fully understood.

But Providence at a certain point thought he had borne enough, at least for the time being, and sent him the wonderful gift of Padre Eusebio. On top of what he signified for Padre Pio, never had there been in the monastery a friar who endeared himself more to all and sundry by his holiness, his wit, his kindliness, his intelligence and his dynamism. Never before had it happened that, with Padre Pio still alive, whole busloads of people from San Giovanni journeyed at the weekend to see again a friar who had been transferred elsewhere.

The photograph I have mentioned and the tale I have told of the Sunday morning episode in the "Choir" are sufficient synopsis of all he meant to the suffering, saintly old man whom he worshiped.

Padre Pio was now not only the special kind of martyr he had been all his life; he was also an old man, with the ailments and disabilities of age added to his other sufferings. He needed understanding and devoted attention now more than ever; and he got it from Padre Eusebio.

As had been the case with Dr. Sanguinetti, there existed in Padre Eusebio the deepest underlying veneration for Padre Pio to motivate his outlook and actions, and that again was supplemented by a total confidence and spontaneity which other people never quite achieved. I suppose it sprang from utter lack of vanity, complete forgetfulness of self, and entire dedication. No matter how well one got to know Padre Pio, undoubtedly for the lack of some of these qualities there remained always an element of constraint in his presence.

But Padre Eusebio restored to him the comfort and support and light that he had lost. He could coax him into taking more care of himself, he could joke him out of his bouts of weariness or depression, and day and night he was always available, always there. Not only the friars and people of San Giovanni loved him for that and for his own happy, unselfish disposition, but we who came there to visit sensed these things at once and grew to appreciate them more and more as the years passed. We came away from San Giovanni content in the knowledge that, so long as Padre Eusebio was there, Padre Pio, humanly speaking, was all right.

After some happy years of this situation, ecclesiastical clouds began to gather again over the monastery. A new General from the States found the Order in several parts of Italy not up to form. Some friars in Sicily had become embroiled with the Mafia, probably with the best of intentions by trying to mediate; others were found to be involved in cigarette smuggling; many houses of the Order had lost funds through investing them with a super-optimist named Giuffre, called "The Banker of God." (Padre Pio had not endeared himself to certain Superiors by refusing to allow hospital funds to be used as a stop-gap for these losses.)

I suppose the new General thought, like others before him, that the situation in San Giovanni was highly unorthodox and might get out of hand. So off we went again with vexatious investigations, demands for strict adherence to the normal monastery rules, hostile interrogation of the friars, and the order to some of them to report confidentially and directly back. An unhappy time it was for Padre Pio, for the Community, and for the life of San Giovanni as a whole.

However, Padre Pio could have weathered these rough times too, as he had done in the past. But then the blow fell. Padre Eusebio was to be transferred. This was incredible news. All of us who knew the situation and the effect this was bound to have on Padre Pio asked ourselves why and how such a heartless decision could ever have been taken.

Eventually I found out, when discussing the matter in the Vatican, that jealousy and resentment on the part of certain lay "collaborators" had played a leading part. In a complete travesty of the truth, Padre Eusebio had been accused of making himself a barrier between Padre Pio and those who came to see him.

Poor Padre Pio! It was too much for him. He folded up under the blow. And little wonder. The slightest sense of gratitude or appreciation, the smallest bit of human compassion, not alone for one tired and broken as he was in the service of God, but for an old and sick man, should have saved him from it. He thought the time had come for him to depart.

I thought so too when I saw him lying in his cell. He was in a deplorable state, obviously running a high temperature, bathed in sweat, with his morale lower than I had ever seen it.

I fear that holy cell was defiled on this occasion by some irate, harsh, and uncharitable thoughts, though maybe it was a case of being angry and sinning not. The sight would have made the angels weep. As I was leaving, I told him I was going to the Vatican. He did not try to stop me. "Tell them," he said in a dispirited voice, "that if they want to put me in the tomb, this is the shortest road."

It was a long time since I had been in the Vatican; not since the days of Pius XII, whom I knew well. But I managed to present the case to Cardinal Antoniutti, head of the Congregation for Religious, who was most sympathetic; to Monsignor Macchi, Pope Paul's personal secretary; and to Monsignor Mauro, who was put in charge of the inquiries. The upshot was that a letter was addressed to me by

Cardinal Dall'Acqua, from the cordial and under-standing text of which it seemed that Padre Eusebio would have his transfer rescinded.

It never happened. I was told later that a decision to intervene in this sense had been taken, but before it could be implemented a person well known and respected in Vatican circles had arrived after a visit to San Giovanni, where he had been primed by those originally responsible for the transfer, and had repeated their thesis. The Vatican was nonplussed and, understandably in the circumstances, decided not to exert any pressure.

However, by whatever kindly inspiration, if Padre Eusebio was not sent back to Padre Pio—and he was as near irreplaceable as makes no matter—his place was at least taken by one than whom none could have been more suitable. This was Padre Pellegrino, of whom I shall speak in the following chapter.

Meanwhile, a sad and disconsolate Padre Eusebio had been sent on a species of traveling holiday, visiting houses of his Order in various countries. In the course of it he came to Ireland, where we succeeded in having him with us for a weekend in Donegal. It was something unforgettable to see the friar and friend we had known only in San Giovanni and alongside Padre Pio saying Mass in the village church of Mountcharles and sitting around a turf fire with us in the evening. We felt that Padre Pio had sent him to us as a special mark of friendship; and seated around that fire we knew that, as Emanuele Brunatto had said at Grenoble, we were not alone.

To finish this chapter on Padre Eusebio, here is a small tale involving him. Like so many others, it is interesting only because of its protagonist; but, having accepted that, I think it is a pleasant one.

One day in the monastery Padre Pio and he were having a semi-serious argument. Padre Pio turned to me in appeal and said, "Listen to him! You agree with *me,* don't you?" "No, Padre," I replied. "I agree with *him!*" He looked at me in amazement, while his opponent gave an exclamation of triumph. "What do I hear? You agree with Padre Eusebio?" "Yes, indeed, for I have heard it said that it is better to have a friend at court than to know the king!" With amazing, unsuspected force he pinned my shoulders against the corridor wall and said, "If ever you make a remark like that again, do you know what is going to happen to you?" "No, Padre, I don't! And what's more, I don't want to—I won't!" He accepted the unconditional surrender and released me, wagging an admonitory finger.

CHAPTER XLVII

Padre Pellegrino was, as I have said, the friar called to take Padre Eusebio's place. He had been in San Giovanni for a number of years before then, and though during that first period I never had had much conversation with him, he had made a strong impression upon me. He was extremely reserved, with a ready smile, but one that came from within, so to speak. He always seemed as though he had just made his ablutions and brushed his habit. His whole aspect and demeanor proclaimed a self-discipline that one guessed was partly natural and partly acquired. One felt that—always pleasantly, with courtesy, but nonetheless wholly—he would always be his own man.

Padre Eusebio's make-up was spontaneous, emotional, and extrovert. To be given the task of looking after Padre Pio, and thus to be so much in the public eye, did not worry him in the slightest. He took to it like a duck to water. On the other hand, when I got to know Padre Pellegrino, I easily imagined to what anxieties, doubts, and perplexities the walls of his cell must often have been witness when he took on that, for him, daunting task.

However, he too had the greatest possible veneration for Padre Pio; he was sensitive and tactful, and adding to that his obvious resolve to serve God and St. Francis to the best of his ability, no better substi-

tute than Padre Pellegrino could have been found.
He would never twit Padre Pio affectionately or
make him laugh, or insist on his doing this or that
for his own good; but he too would always be there,
day and night, serious, attentive, and sympathetic.
And after all, it was he that Providence had chosen
or allowed to be in attendance on Padre Pio at a
most serious moment in his life, the most serious
moment of all, that of his passing from among us.

Padre Pellegrino spoke to me on a number of occasions of his life in his new role, of episodes that
took place, of things Padre Pio had said or done.
But all that has now disappeared from my mind.
Now when I think of Padre Pellegrino, I have no
longer a picture of him chatting in his cell, or
seriously intent on his devotions in the choir stalls,
or moving around San Giovanni with his air of quiet
reserve. He has become for always the man who was
with Padre Pio when his fifty-year Calvary ended;
and I see him alone with him, witnessing his last actions and hearing his last words.

There was no real indication of approaching
death. On that last day he had appeared weary and
ill, but he had so often been that way before. Dr.
Sala, Gino Ghisleri's son-in-law, who was his doctor
at the time, told me there was no evident reason why
he should have died then rather than at any time
since he had known him.

It had to be that way; for half a century there was
no good natural reason why he should have remained alive. All that happened now was that God
removed from his body that supernatural strength
which kept his great soul within it. The end of his

incredible sufferings had been decreed, and he was beckoned to his reward.

It was not altogether correct to say that there was no indication of his approaching death. The coming termination of his passion was manifested some time before, when his stigmata gradually began to disappear. But if he himself realized the significance of this, he told no one openly.

It was one of the most shattering experiences I ever had, to be called to the telephone one morning and be given the news, out of the blue, of his death. It was like a hammer blow on the head. I could not believe it.

It was at the end of an intense day, when there had been a great gathering of the Prayer Groups at San Giovanni. Padre Pellegrino was sitting up with him but was not unduly anxious.

Strange things began to happen, however. Padre Pio asked to make his confession. Afterward he repeated his act of religious profession. He then requested Padre Pellegrino if he would ask pardon on his behalf for any offense he might ever have given to other members of the Community. He furthermore asked him if he would convey his blessing to his spiritual sons and daughters and to his relatives. He asked a surprising question at that still early hour (it was not long after midnight): "Have you said Mass yet?" he inquired. To the astonished negative response of Padre Pellegrino he gave the reply "This morning you will say it for me." Padre Pellegrino assured him that he said Mass each day for his intentions (which, with the Guardian's permission, he did).

Even then he was not aware, or anyhow con-

vinced, of the drama at which he was assisting; all
the more so since shortly afterward Padre Pio got out
of bed with his assistance, put on his habit, and
suggested going to the little terrace for a breath of
air.

At that point another strange thing happened.
Though severely afflicted by arthritis and having either to be helped along or transported in a wheel
chair, he now strode easily along the corridor and
himself switched on the terrace light. Padre Pellegrino said nothing, for he was accustomed to strange
things happening. But after some five minutes, during which they sat there quietly and Padre Pio had
looked around him, he began to be worried, for
when they rose to return Padre Pio's strength
seemed to have left him almost completely, and he
had to be helped into his wheel chair, and then with
considerable difficulty onto a chair in his cell.

After that events moved quickly. Padre Pio was
now pale, his brow was bathed in perspiration, and
he began softly to repeat the names of Jesus and
Mary.

Padre Pellegrino was by now thoroughly alarmed,
and he made for the door to call the Father Guardian. He was halted by a request, given in firm tones,
to disturb no one. However, as Padre Pio's breathing became heavier and he sat there with eyes
closed, still repeating the names of Jesus and Mary,
he paid no attention to a second attempt to stop him
but awakened the Guardian and also Brother Bill,
who sometimes shared his watches. He then tele-
phoned urgently for Dr. Sala.

When he got back to the cell it was clearer than
ever that this was no ordinary crisis, and he tele-

phoned to the hospital, whence Dr. Gusso and another doctor arrived with all possible speed to join Dr. Sala.

The three doctors did all they could to prevent the total collapse which they saw to be imminent, but it was all to no avail. The Community were roused, and as they knelt there, shocked, saying the prayers for the dying, Padre Pio passed serenely from among them. Dr. Gusso said afterward it was the most serene passing he had ever witnessed.

He died as he had lived, wearing his habit, with the rosary beads held in his fingers and with the two beloved names of Jesus and Mary on his lips. For him too Christ had said His *"consummatum est,"* and the long passion was over.

It is my firm belief that God raised up this servant of His as a last appeal and warning to mankind before they should plunge themselves into unspeakable catastrophe. Is it too late for us to follow the men of Nineveh and repent? Christ spread His message and His goodness during His life, but it was after His death that the real fruits of His divine mission to mankind were accomplished. So also can it be now, if we pay heed to and emulate His servant. Padre Pio can still help us to avoid both individual and universal catastrophe, if we give him the chance.

CHAPTER XLVIII

The tales are not yet over. Some time previously the BBC had expressed a desire to make a film on Padre Pio. It was to be produced by a young man named Mischa Scorer; and against all the probabilities Padre Pio, generally averse to this type of publicity, had consented—not to be interviewed—but, as part of the film, to let shots be taken in church while he was saying Mass. It was like a legacy that he was leaving behind him.

Mischa Scorer, who is a perfectionist, made a superb documentary into which went a large amount of patient research and some beautiful photography. The research emerged in the selection of people interviewed; and it was from these interviews that Padre Pio and his work chiefly emerged in their turn. The film was all the better for its being done by someone who was not a Catholic, and completely objective in his approach. It was cool and detached; and this only threw into greater relief the human setting for Padre Pio's amazing miracles; his warmth, his compassion and what we might call his holy, dedicated normality.

The film won an award at Monte Carlo, was shown on both BBC channels, and has been given at least twice by RTE.

The portion done at San Giovanni had its own characteristic story inset. When the lamps were set up in the church the night before for the shots of the Mass, there was one playing directly on the altar in such a way that it could hardly have failed to distract the celebrant. The technicians, however, using their own criteria, decided to leave it that way. Next morning when the lamps were switched on, all of them functioned perfectly except that one. Padre Pio was not going to have his Mass disturbed.

This was recounted to me by Mischa Scorer himself—the episode, I mean, not the interpretation, which is mine.

He thought, when we were speaking, that his main work was over and that what mostly remained now was the task of cutting and editing. He was mistaken. The film was to be more complete than that. When he was about to leave Rome for London, he received the news of Padre Pio's death, and some of the most moving, powerful scenes were those of Padre Pio's body lying in a glass-covered coffin while masses of people filed by, kissing the glass above his face as they passed—and, of course, those of the funeral itself. It was a finished documentation of the life and death of what the film's title termed him: "A Very Private Man."

If Padre Carmelo da Sessano, the former Father Guardian, was unsuccessful with his attempts at recording conversations, at least his televising of the Mass at the inauguration of the hospital created a precedent and, together with the above and with at least two other documentaries, one American and one Swiss, has ensured that future generations will see Padre Pio as he was, will see the places and the people that were background and vehicle for his mission, will hear first hand some fascinating ac-

counts from a wide variety of people of the extraordinary things that befell them, and will be able to
witness, above all, that most impressive spectacle, his
Holy Mass.

CHAPTER XLIX

I have said practically nothing of that Mass of Padre Pio in itself. Here, partly to remedy that, is the substance of the script which Radio Eireann was prevented from broadcasting more than twenty years ago. It attempts briefly to describe it, and also the world of San Giovanni in general.

Padre Pio

In the two thousand years of the Church's history many miracles have happened. That history opened with the biggest miracle of all, which is the Incarnation. It continues today with the universal daily miracle of the Mass and of the Real Presence in tabernacles all over the globe.

Besides these fundamental, continuous and accepted miracles, there have been right down the ages examples of miracles worked by the intercession of holy men and women. Our whole religious history is full of them, and today, before the Church will raise a person to her altars and proclaim him or her a saint, she imposes the condition that two clear and authenticated miracles will have been brought about through his or her intercession *after* death.

In other words, that Church which has given to the world its most exalted thinkers and men of science sees no difficulty at all in accepting that God, who made the wondrous succession of laws which govern nature in this finite and three-dimensional world of ours, can if He wishes dispense with those laws. She really sees nothing more wonderful in the interruption of the law than in its amazing existence and continuity. And what we call a miracle, in fact, is in itself no greater manifestation of God's power than the most banal normality. Its real significance lies in the effect it produces upon our own blunted minds and senses.

Naturally the Church, being not only divinely founded and inspired, but being also the oldest, most experienced, and wisest institution in the world today, has learned always to move slowly, never to decide rashly, and always to be ready for delusions in the behavior of mortal man, possessor as he is until the moment of his death of a free will, and subject as he is to human weakness and temptation. Furthermore, she has no essential need, in herself, of these spectacular, sporadic interruptions of the natural laws which we call miracles. She stands foursquare and complete without them, and so can afford to be as cautious and completely detached in her approach to them as she would be in the consideration of something like, say, Einstein's theory of relativity.

Nonetheless, though the Church will not identify herself with any individual or with specifically individual manifestations during the life of the person concerned, for the reasons already stated, we know that the saints become saints during their lifetime, not after their death, that the miracles they worked or which were worked upon their persons took place while they were still alive, and that she would not have asked any of those privileged to witness such manifestations to take no notice of them or to pretend that they had not been aware of them. Further, I will go so far as to say that, knowing the facts of the lives of the canonized saints, we could not now imagine any of them, once they had embarked upon their career of sanctity, going astray before death, for the very good reason that they had so surrendered their free will into the hands of God that God could never let them down.

I used the phrase "worked upon their persons." That was a reference to what is known as the stigmata, the marks of Christ's Passion reproduced upon a living human body. There have been about sixty accepted instances of this in the Church's history, the best known being the stigmata of St. Francis of Assisi. And that brings us to our present subject, Padre Pio of Pietralcina, an Italian Capuchin priest of seventy-two years of age who for over thirty years has borne in his body the five wounds of Christ, and of whom thousands of rational, cold-thinking people will testify that he is not only the holiest man they have ever met but that he has been the channel of innumerable preternatural manifestations in their regard.

I have had the very great privilege of visiting Padre Pio on a number of occasions, of coming into direct contact with some of those manifestations, and I would testify with the utmost certainty to their preternatural nature and furthermore give it as my personal conviction that Padre Pio, living among us today, is one of the saintliest men, possessing and using the most astounding powers, that ever trod the face of the earth. These words come from one whom no one would ever describe as having the slightest tendency toward either mysticism or emotionalism. I am presently occupied in very ordinary business activities and my whole background and make-up are such that the first time I went to see Padre Pio, ten years after I had first heard of him, I did so almost reluctantly and, as it were, constrained by a peculiar chain of circumstances which it would be here irrelevant to relate.

During those ten preceding years a number of people in various walks of life had spoken to me of Padre Pio. Some of them were men for whose intelligence I had the deepest respect. One of them was the most intelligent and erudite man I know; and through them I knew the broad outlines of Padre Pio's life and attributes. He was a Capuchin priest, born of peasant parents in one of the poorest and most remote regions of southern Italy. He had been noted from early youth for his strength of character, his extreme piety, and his generous, warm nature. His life had been passed almost completely in small houses of the Order, and ever since he had been marked with the stigmata he had lived in an extremely small monastery, right out in the wilds, about a mile or so from the village of San Giovanni Rotondo, which in turn is roughly an hour's journey by car or bus from the nearest railroad station of Foggia, a five-hour train journey south from Rome and on the Adriatic side of the peninsula.

Despite his sanctity and the amazing gifts attributed to him, the Church was obviously running true to form, and so far from drawing any attention to him was leaving him buried in his wilderness precisely like any of his fellow monks. Indeed she had gone further. For almost a decade his Superiors had segregated him from any priestly public contact, an imposition accepted with the same tranquility by Padre Pio as he accepted its termination and his present tremendously wearing life of continuous contact with the hundreds of thousands of people who from one year's end to another bring him without a day, almost without an hour, of respite their burdens and their sorrows both spiritual and physical.

I knew he converted sinners, healed the sick, that he was asserted to possess the extreme gift of bilocation, which is to say, able to be present elsewhere without ever physically leaving his monastery; that his wounds bled continuously, that the blood and the wounds on occasion gave out a strong and beautiful perfume which manifested itself not only in his presence but was often, for some special reason, felt with equal strength and distinctness by persons who were hundreds or thousands of miles away.

All these things I knew from those friends and acquaintances who had visited Padre Pio. Then, after taking the decision to go and visit him myself, I collected most of the literature which had been published concerning him and went through it. All of it was obviously written by people of good faith, but much of it was marred by emotionalism and in some cases by superstition on the part of the authors; and with one exception all of these books were shortly afterward banned by the Vatican, which, however, lifted its ban on revised editions of the most sensible ones.

That exception referred to above was the one which then made most appeal to me. It was over two hundred pages of medical analyses and investigations by a well-known Roman doctor who had been given the task of examining and finding if possible a human biological or perhaps pathological explanation of the stigmata. The doctor began in the most detached and objective manner possible. His investigations and his examination of every single human hypothesis covered a considerable period. He ended completely objective as he began, but no longer detached. All hypotheses had to be discarded in the light of his painstaking observations and tests, and only one answer remained. It was that the phenomenon had no human explanation; and the professor too became a fervent disciple of the man he had so thoroughly and meticulously sifted.

Notwithstanding all the above, I still went down to San Giovanni with my normal mental reactions and outlook putting up a battle against the weight of secondhand evidence. I was the doubting Thomas. But after twenty-four hours there I not only had not one shred of resistance left but had become in my turn one of Padre Pio's most humble and convinced admirers.

Was he hypnotic? Did he direct the force of a dramatic personality upon me? Was he away up in the clouds, to be gazed at with awe and trepidation? Not at all. The most striking and lovable things about Padre Pio in one's conversations with him are his warm, normal humanity, his great kindliness, and his sense of humor. But the sanctity and suffering of Padre Pio shine through him of themselves. And the effect upon all those who come in contact with him is a combination of affection and of veneration in just about equal deep measure.

It is customary still to talk of going to San Giovanni Rotondo; but in actual fact one passes through it and goes right on to what now amounts to another small village that has grown up in recent years around the monastery itself; and one finds accommodation in one of the hotels or boardinghouses that the needs of the unceasing stream of pilgrims have created. These have no connection with the monastery but are run soberly and decently by people who have settled there spontaneously. Alongside them are other private houses built by persons who have given up their ordinary way of life to be beside Padre Pio and in most cases to help him in his works of spiritual and temporal mercy. Dominating everything is the huge, architecturally striking, white hospital which has arisen by wish of Padre Pio, supported by charitable contributions from all over the world, built by an architect never university-trained and possessing no degree, beautiful in conception, most modern in its layout and equipment, and destined for the relief of the suffering no matter who they are or whence they come.

One generally arrives in the evening. It is a long and exacting journey for most people; and one goes early to bed, for Padre Pio says his Mass at five o'clock each morning, and that means rising around four.

It is something unforgettable, the walk up under the stars in the cold darkness of the early morning to the little church of Santa Maria delle Grazie. The stillness, the other dim groups of figures making their way up, and the unworldly atmosphere of the occasion contrast strongly with the bustling materialistic world from which one has so recently come.

Masses are beginning at other altars, but the great crowd is around the altar dedicated to St. Francis whither Padre Pio will soon make his way, moving with difficulty through the packed people, not smiling or jovial now, but as though weary and weighed down with all the suffering and sorrow of the world.

For Padre Pio's life has centered around the Passion of Our Lord, and in his preparation for the Mass and his celebration of it is concentrated more than in anything else that chief motive power of his whole existence, the accompanying of his Divine Master in His sufferings.

It is difficult to speak of that Mass. It is impossible to describe it adequately. It has to be experienced. But for more than an hour one is held spellbound by the deep intensity with which it is said; not a physical intensity, for his movements are slow and deliberate, his voice full and low-pitched, but an intensity of the spirit wherein we now glimpse a Padre Pio obviously inhabiting a world other than the material world around him; at times clearly suffering, at times as though looking on things unseen by us, at times in apparent mental converse; through all and above all his evident tremendous consciousness of the significance of his words and actions; and there, clearly revealed, the bleeding perforations in his hands. In a way, when you have seen his Mass, you have seen everything, or at least you fully understand and accept everything.

That Mass is the beginning of his public day. It is a day that would massacre any strong man sustaining himself on the most invigorating of diets. Padre Pio eats once a day, under obedience, and takes not as much as would sustain an infant. Yet as often as I have met him at the end of the day he has looked fresher, more lightsome and cheerful than at the beginning.

He confesses daily for five or six solid hours. During the rest of it he finds time to give Communion at half past ten in the morning to all those, and they are always many, who wish to communicate at

his hands; sometimes to give Benediction; sometimes
to baptize; to attend to the spiritual requirements of
the other monks, of whom he is the spiritual director; and above all to see and speak with as many as
possible of those hosts of people who have come
from far and near to receive comfort from him. He
is under continuous assault. They surround him in
the sacristy. They await his exits from the confessional, his passings from church to monastery and
back. They seek a word, a blessing, from him for
themselves or for others. They hold out their children to him. They ask his blessing on the religious
objects they have brought with them. They obtain
meetings with him in the bare monastery parlor, in
the monastery corridors and, in the case of the
women, in the public corridor separating monastery
and church.

This is a strain which no normal man could with-
stand for even a limited period of time, yet it has
been going on with increasing momentum for tens of
long years, day in and day out, without interruption.
The only moments he has to himself are during the
brief night in his cell, and one can well guess that
great part of those too are spent in prayer, meditation, intimate union with God, and intercession, always intercession, for others.

Did I speak of miracles? Is not that existence in
itself a miracle? But why be reticent, why hide it?
The place is literally teeming with miracles. Month
after month there appear in the Italian press sensational detailed reports of cures effected through him.
A striking one which I remember is that of a child
who had fallen from a window and had its skull
fractured in four places with protrusion of brain tis-

sue. It was healed instantly. Then there is a girl, now twenty years of age, who was born blind, for her eyes had no pupils in them. At the age of six she was given her sight by Padre Pio and has retained it ever since. She still has no pupils.

In my own office some time ago I had a call from three men met at San Giovanni Rotondo: one had been blind, another a desperate case of cancer of the throat, and a third was one of Italy's leading stage and film comedians. The man who had been blind now sat looking at me. His eyes, which had been like shriveled peas, were now completely reformed. The man with the throat cancer, who had been able to speak only in an almost inaudible whisper when I knew him first, and in whose throat a tube had been inserted, now sat talking animatedly and smoking American cigarettes. The third man, at a certain point in the conversation, astounded all of us by stating bluntly that he had had the biggest cure of all. "Your cancer of the throat," said he, "was only child's play compared with mine, for mine was very deep-rooted. It was cancer of the soul."

In the course of my visits to San Giovanni I have met people, serious and intelligent people, to whom Padre Pio has appeared. I have met others to whom he has revealed their past lives, their most secret preoccupations, their sins, at a first meeting.

It is a commonplace for him in the confessional to remind his penitents of some sin they have forgotten, or to refuse to hear the confessions of others who have later admitted that they were not in the proper dispositions. I have met Communists and atheists who have been attracted down there by some strange message or compulsion, in one case by a direct apparition and spoken message, and who have become converted to lives of exemplary Christianity and in some cases of great personal sacrifice. I have known of people who have been assisted on their deathbeds by Padre Pio. Of these last cases, one took place in South America and one in the United States. The instances of people who have felt the strong characteristic perfume, the literal odor of sanctity, that I have already spoken of, are legion. I have felt it myself without the slightest possibility of error or autosuggestion, both in the presence of Padre Pio and at hundreds of miles' distance, alone and in the company of others.

Let me emphasize one thing. I have made many friends through these journeys to see Padre Pio. Some are monks; some are priests; some are among those marvelous people who have given up their profession, their industry, their job, their home, to live permanently alongside Padre Pio and participate in his labors; some were visitors like myself. In all cases they are sane, common-sense people, most of them, I found, with a good sense of humor, which I mention specifically because it generally springs from a sound sense of proportion. None of them are neurotics. All of them are bound by one common tie: they worship the ground Padre Pio walks on.

In a multitude of cases that warm affection and profound veneration which they conceived for him at San Giovanni has been transplanted and has blossomed forth in numerous groups known as Friends of Padre Pio, who in Rome, New York, Buenos Aires, London, and in towns and villages scattered across the Western world meet at least once a month to assist at a Mass offered for his intentions and to pray for an hour in union with him. In Milan, several such groups have banded together and a Mass attended by a number of group members is celebrated in the cathedral for his intentions on every day of the year.

Let me give the reactions of some interesting people. In the monastery parlor hangs a photograph of a cardinal archbishop. Beneath it in his own hand is his request for Padre Pio's prayers for him and for his archdiocese.

An ex-Communist said the following to me: "Since my conversion (through contact with Padre Pio) I have read many saints' lives. It has seemed to me that their degree of sanctity corresponded to the measure in which they resembled Christ Himself. It is this Christlike quality in Padre Pio which attracts me to him so strongly." He could hardly have synthesized things better or more truly.

Considering all these things, we may well be led to ask ourselves what is the significance of a figure like Padre Pio in the world today. It is not perhaps unduly difficult to find an answer. Our world puts the accent upon its modernity, prides itself on its advancement. That is really very stupid. Living men have always been modern. They have always been able to point to their advancement. But twenty years later they were considered to be back numbers, for the next generation had discovered yet more of the material treasure house that had always existed, merely awaiting discovery, in God's creation.

However, drunk with the truly great rapidity and extent of recent such discovery, our generation have outdone themselves in mistaken vanity and blindness, and we have attained a pathetic and suicidal substitution of achievement-worship which no previous generation since the foundation of Christianity has equaled. The alleged splendor of the works of man, material, intellectual, social, and political, is superimposed upon the real splendor of creation. And the result is the noonday darkness of our present situation.

In that darkness Padre Pio, the lowly monk, is a beacon: a beacon which has already pierced the darkness far and wide, and which, in the humble opinion of many like myself, is destined to cast its rays upon the entire world.

Padre Pio has not moved out into the world. He remains in his remote wilderness, clad in the rough medieval garb of his Order, following the precepts laid down by Francis in the thirteenth century, giving complete obedience to his Superiors. But the world comes to him increasingly, by all the modern means of transport, overland, on the sea, and in the air. It comes, not as modern man, but only as man, the everlasting man, in need of comfort, enlightenment, and inspiration. And no one goes empty-handed away.

Men have recorded his voice as he recited the Rosary in the little church, and it has been broadcast on our lately discovered sound waves to the ends of the earth. But there are other and stronger waves going out incessantly from San Giovanni across the earth. They enable one to regard the world and its problems with truer vision, with equanimity, and with deepened responsibility; which is a way of saying with reawakened faith, hope, and charity. From the beacon of Padre Pio, indeed, may come a blaze of light and warmth that will restore humanity.

CHAPTER L

The foregoing chapter is more or less a synthesis or explanation of the rest of the book; a curious one since it was written so long ago, before the book was conceived or the material for it available.

The moment has now come to conclude, but before doing so I want to recount yet another tale, and this time a cautionary one.

Once when my wife and I were down at San Giovanni Rotondo, I had the privilege of serving Padre Pio's Mass in the old church at the altar of St. Francis. During the Mass two children were to receive their first Holy Communion, and when they had done so, their parents too received Communion from his hands. After that there came a group of women whom I took to be close relatives, and, instead of going forward in my turn, I stayed kneeling at the side of the altar. At length only one Host remained in the small ciborium and, taking it, Padre Pio turned to me and said, "Aren't you going to Communion?" "Yes, Padre," I answered. He then motioned me to come forward; I realized later that the communicants had not been relatives but members of the redoubtable "Holy Women," or other such rugged characters.

The incident had been duly noted, and after Mass when my wife and I were walking down to the hotel, what I can perhaps best describe as three old female battle-axes fell in behind us. One of them remarked somewhat brashly, "Well, *signore,* you were very lucky this morning!" I made some noncommittal reply but was immediately submerged in a stream of comment and interrogation, especially interrogation. They rapidly elicited the fact that we were foreigners, and our original interlocutor exclaimed, "Ah, foreigners, are you? See what we've got in Italy!" I could not resist the low temptation and made the wicked rejoinder: "But perhaps, ladies, that is because you need it so badly!"

There is a present moral to that small episode. It is that just as the three women and most of the rest of us found ourselves at San Giovanni, not because we were holy or worthy of it, but often for diametrically opposite reasons, so the fact that one writes a book about Padre Pio is no guarantee of any worthiness to be associated with him. On the contrary, the fact that such a person as the author writes such a book is but one more proof that Padre Pio, like his Master, came not just for the naturally good but also and especially for the black sheep of the flock. This is something which I should like to be thoroughly understood.

Like the Church, he was and is there chiefly for those who need help and guidance, rather than for those who don't. And in order to help, he had to be close to us, to be able fully to understand us and our difficulties.

It is my hope that from these simple tales there will emerge the figure of a man, martyred all his life, yes, as no mere human being was ever martyred before; but generous, compassionate, understanding, humorous: definitely one of us.

As on earth he was no dweller in an ivory tower, neither is he remotely inaccessible in heaven. Now as then he is sympathetically aware of our limitations, our needs, and our weak-willed aspirations.

Despite his great gifts and powers, and remembering them, let my readers think of him as being there alongside them to help them in their trials or difficulties. If they truly desire it, that is exactly where they will find him.

If these stories don't tell that, they have told nothing.

CHAPTER LI

No book about Padre Pio would be complete without reference to one who, after God, was the great love of his life. I refer to Our Lady. "There are people so foolish," he said, "that they think they can go through life without the help of the Madonna."

I have never understood the unwillingness on the part of non-Catholics to venerate her who was chosen to be the human mother of God made man. Surely if God so loved and respected her, we must do likewise. If we treasure the love of an earthly mother, we should look with even greater affection and veneration upon her who has been vouchsafed to us as a heavenly mother. And if we prize and honor a portrait of one, is it not logical and no slightest sign of superstition to erect statues and create paintings in honor of the other? If it is better to have a friend at court than to know the king, isn't it a thousand times better to have a mother there?

This is the last tale in the book. It is not mine but Padre Pio's own, as I heard him recount it.

One day, he said, Christ was walking with St. Peter through Paradise. Suddenly He became aware of the presence of a number of villainous-looking individuals who seemed to Him completely out of place there. "Look!" he said to St. Peter. "How did these people get in?" "Nothing to do with me!" answered St. Peter. "You must ask Your mother. Every time she finds my back turned, she opens the gates and lets *everybody* in!"

GLOSSARY

The following terms may need some explanation for the general reader: they are given here in alphabetical order.

Angelus A brief prayer said daily in Roman Catholic environments at noon and at 6 P.M., signaled by the ringing of church bells.

Benediction A religious service in which the congregation is blessed by the Blessed Sacrament held aloft by the priest and moved in the Sign of the Cross.

Bi-location A word devised to account for events which seem to imply the ability to be in two places at once.

Blessed Sacrament Strictly speaking, the Eucharist. Here used to mean a host consecrated at Mass and kept for the Communion of the sick, for Benediction, or for use in procession.

Capuchin A member of one of the religious orders which traces its origin to St. Francis of Assisi.

Confessional A place designed for the reception of the sacrament of penance in its private form. There is commonly a movable shutter between priest and penitent.

Consecration That part of the Mass in which the bread and wine are blessed and their "substance" as the body and blood of Christ is declared.

Excommunication Exclusion from membership of the Church.

Father Guardian The friar in charge of a Capuchin community.

Host In general, the unleavened bread used in the Mass, commonly a small round white wafer. Here means a consecrated host.

Litany of Loreto A form of public prayer, often sung, which stresses the role of the Blessed Virgin.

Monstrance A large receptacle, usually decorated, in which the consecrated host is placed for Benediction and eucharistic processions.

Oratory Chapel used for common and private prayer.

Real presence I.e., of the body and blood of Christ in the eucharistic elements.

Repositories Shops for the sale of pious objects and books.

Rosary Traditional form of prayer involving the use of beads.

Stigmatist Someone who has in his body wounds similar to the wounds which are likely to have been suffered by Jesus of Nazareth when he was crucified. St. Francis of Assisi is said to have been one.

Tabernacle A small receptacle in a church for the preservation of consecrated hosts.

Tonsure A ritual haircut in sign of dedication to God.

Visitation The procedure for investigating the life of a religious community to make sure that all is in order or, if not, to ensure that reforms are made. There is a routine form of visitation at fixed intervals of a few years, but the visitations mentioned here are special or extraordinary, undertaken in response to complaints made to the Roman authorities about Padre Pio or his associates.

John McCaffery was lecturer in English at Genoa University and Director of the British Institute there, 1933–40. During the war he was Chief of Special Operations Europe, the underground organization centered in Switzerland. After the war he went into insurance, banking, and business in Milan. In his early days he was also a journalist. In recent years, and until his death in 1981, John McCaffery had been farming in Donegal, Ireland, though he continued to write.